That's More Of It Now

the second book of
Irish Mammies

COLM O'REGAN

TRANSWORLD IRELAND

TRANSWORLD IRELAND
an imprint of The Random House Group Limited
20 Vauxhall Bridge Road, London SW1V 2SA
www.transworldbooks.co.uk

First published in 2013 by Transworld Ireland,
a division of Transworld Publishers

Copyright © Colm O'Regan 2013

Colm O'Regan has asserted his right under the Copyright, Designs
and Patents Act 1988 to be identified as the author of this work.

Design by Curious Design
Illustrations by Doug Ferris
Photograph on page 149 copyright © The Country Range Group

A CIP catalogue record for this book
is available from the British Library.

ISBN 9781848271760

This book is sold subject to the condition that it shall not,
by way of trade or otherwise, be lent, resold, hired out,
or otherwise circulated without the publisher's prior
consent in any form of binding or cover other than that
in which it is published and without a similar condition,
including this condition, being imposed on the
subsequent purchaser.

Addresses for Random House Group Ltd companies outside the UK
can be found at: www.randomhouse.co.uk
The Random House Group Ltd Reg. No. 954009

The Random House Group Limited supports the Forest Stewardship Council®
(FSC®), the leading international forest-certification organisation. Our books
carrying the FSC label are printed on FSC®-certified paper. FSC is the only
forest-certification scheme supported by the leading environmental organisations,
including Greenpeace. Our paper procurement policy can be found at
www.randomhouse.co.uk/environment

Printed and bound in Great Britain by
Clays Ltd, Bungay, Suffolk

2 4 6 8 10 9 7 5 3 1

Contents

Are your hands clean? … Show me … Go back
out now and wash them likeagoodchild.

Introduction

Welcome to the second book of Irish Mammies. As you can see from the cover, you've arrived just in time for the tea.

For those of you who've just joined us, a quick recap. *Isn't It Well for Ye?* was the first book and it was inspired by the popularity of the @irishmammies Twitter account — which by this stage has gathered in more than 100,000 followers. The first book was bought by different types of people: Mammies curious to see what the fuss was about, people interested to find out if every family had a good scissors and quite a lot of people who bought it in a panic just before the shop closed on Christmas Eve. Whoever they were, it seems that at least some readers enjoyed it, judging from the nice messages they send.

This book tries to cover a few things which the first book might have missed. It gives some must-know information on several important and weighty topics, such as The Vest (the final element in the anti-cold quartet, along with Coats, Cough Bottle and Common Sense), the new pope and the phenomenon of Mammies on a Train.

But it also looks a little more deeply at Mammies' socializing. It hints at a juicy past and pays tribute to the Mammies of all ages who are rushed off their feet, as they try to keep today's youngsters entertained. They are up the walls but if you'll have a bit of patience, they'll be over to you in a second.

Unfortunately, a lot of Mammies' children have had to go abroad. Mammies are delighted they found a bit of work but you might give them a quick call. They have to find out all the news from Facebook and you know they have reservations about that.

That's More of It Now also tries to reflect the fact that Mammies are more than familiar with the new technology and will use it, where appropriate. In fact they could do with even more innovation. So innovators – what's keeping you? To get you started, this book has some suggestions for Mammy-specific software.

When you look at the organizational nous, the high performance under pressure and the results achieved, you come to the inevitable conclusion that the best way forward for Ireland is a government of Mammies.

Above all, this book tries to continue where the first left off – celebrating the wit, wisdom, pragmatism and warmth of an Irish Mammy. It's still very well for us.

Colm O'Regan

Mammy's Turn

Is it a year since the first book? Well 'Magine That. Where did the year go to at all? But I suppose as long as we have our health.

I know I wrote some bit of a thing for the first book. I can't remember what it was to be honest with you, but wasn't I inside in Roches Stores — of course it's not Roches now, some other crowd took it over — and this woman comes up to me and says she, 'You were dead right about the coat.' Says I, 'What coat?' Says she, 'In the book you told us to bring a coat with us in case it rained — and would you believe,' says she, 'didn't I do that and didn't it teem down out of the heavens?'

There you go now.

Anyway, where was I? Oh yes … this second book. Well I heard he was writing it so says I, 'I'll ring him up now while 'tis fresh in my mind because otherwise I'd forget.' I got him on the phone — and that wasn't easy because he's as BUSY — and says I, 'Whatever you do in this oul second book, will you give A Mention to those poor Mammies, rushed off their feet, going here and there, and a lot of them with their own jobs as well. They've far more to be doing than I have and a lot more to worry about besides tea-towels, I can tell you. So I hope he included that now. I'd say he will. He's a good lad despite it all.

It's been a busy year for me too. Didn't I finally get On Line — asthefellasaid. I'd say I was the last one in the country. The woman in the computer class must think I'm an awful eejit but I'll learn at my own pace. Anyway let ye sit over now before the tea gets cold.

You'll have a biscuit, won't you?

Mammy

Mammy, We Hardly Knew You

H … Hello … hello … Oh hello … You were a while answering … It's me … Mammy.

She's back! But who is she really? There are many different variations of Irish mother. Too many to do justice to, even in a tome as weighty as this. But one thing is clear: with such variations in behaviour, language and even anatomy, the Irish Mammy may actually be a different species.

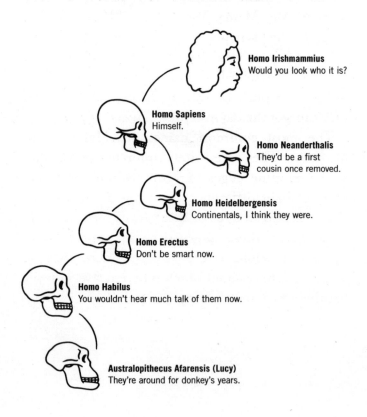

Homo Irishmammius
Would you look who it is?

Homo Sapiens
Himself.

Homo Neanderthalis
They'd be a first
cousin once removed.

Homo Heidelbergensis
Continentals, I think they were.

Homo Erectus
Don't be smart now.

Homo Habilus
You wouldn't hear much talk of them now.

Australopithecus Afarensis (Lucy)
They're around for donkey's years.

Different Strokes

'I don't CARE what the Prendergasts are having for dinner. We're not the Prendergasts.'

But what should we call her?

Mammy, Mam, Mummy, Mum, Mommy, Mom, Mother, Ma, Mama. We all have different names for her. The particular one you use was usually first revealed to your classmates in Senior Infants when you accidentally called your teacher by it instead of 'Miss'. It probably only happened once but you never forgot the day everyone laughed at you.

The most common names are Mammy and Mummy. They are often interchangeable but at the extreme edges of Mummydom, there are ever so slight differences from the Irish Mammy characterized in a lot of this book. Here are some areas where these alternatives in approach are just about visible. (Note — there is absolutely no judgement here about which is better. Every family has their own way of doing things.)

Mummy	Mammy
That hummus is divine.	'Tis gone very humid.
We've just enrolled Cessair in the Little CEOs Club. It's a sort of MBA for tots.	I think he's outside somewhere poking around with a stick.
Darling, you know we've had this conversation. We spoke about your behaviour before when you are faced with a situation which causes you frustration. We said you were to take a deep breath and think about the consequences of what you are doing.	WHATINTHENAMEOF GODAREYOUAFTER DOINGTOYOUR BROTHER?!
We go every year. Nemain loves the whittling in the Body and Soul area.	Whatever you do, stay away from that oul Swedish Mafia House or whatever they're called.
We're going to teach them about all the religions — Buddhism, Islam, Hinduism, Christianity — and Olwen lent us this great new book about the Kabbalah. Then we'll have a secular ceremony instead of communion. Although *my* mother is going to have a fit when she hears.	Ah, will you just do it for me? What am I to say to the neighbours? They'll be wondering why you're not there.

Mummy	Mammy
For Attn: The Principal My daughter Anemone is a pupil in your school. It has come to our attention that one of your teachers instructed her to 'cop on to herself'. We are deeply concerned about the developmental impact this may have on her ...	I was mortified when Miss Mooney told me what you were after getting up to. I'll tell you this much for nothing, there'll be no Jelly Tots this evening, or indeed any evening, for a good while.
So we're thinking Burma this year. Totally unspoiled and a great way for Bruin to practise his naban ... What? Oh, what is it? It's a kind of martial art. I thought it would be good to get him doing some exercise, and you read all the time about this obesity epidemic ...	There we were, all set to go into the Amusements and you got The Runs. And of course your father was no help. All he said was '*I knew well we shouldn't have given him that Mint Aero.*'
It's very important that the children's toys don't impose on them any of the conventional mores of the gung-ho capitalist neo-liberal hegemony.	Who broke your Dinky? ... Who? ... Right, we're going To Sort This Thing Out once and for all ... GETDOWNTHAT STAIRSTHISINSTANT THEPAIROFYE IWANTTOTALKTOYE.
Now, now, Oberon, when you've finished your chia seeds you can have a treat. It's your favourite — we have carob bars!	Sliced pan! How did I forget that? Shur that was the main reason for going in the first place.

There IS a Need for That Kind of Language

'I DID say so. You mustn't have been listening.'

Many Irish Mammies speak a number of tongues, but they have a native language all of their own. On the surface it looks a lot like English but on closer examination you will find a number of tenses, parts of speech and other grammatical quirks that make Irish Mammyish a unique dialect. Whether she's venting frustration or ever-so-gently marking an adult child's cards, the fundamental principle underlying Irish Mammyish is the ability to convey a lot of meaning in very few words.

I don't know WHAT time they'll be finished the silage or will they be wanting The Dinner. } *Future Subjunctive Logistical Tense*

And they wouldn't eat what you'd put in front of them. } *Awkward Conditional Tense*

I was expecting a phone call on Sunday.	*Continuous Present Past Tense*
But I suppose you must have been busy.	*Passive Aggressive Tense*
Sure you're here now anyway. That's the main thing.	*Tense*

In addition to grammatical tension, Irish Mammyish has a number of voices.

- **The Accusative Voice:** Was that you?

- **The Wistful Voice:** Pity you didn't say that earlier and I only just passing the shop.

- **The Elliptical Voice:** I see the Quigleys are expecting their second child ... 'Twouldn't be any harm if ye were getting a move on too.

- **The Understated Voice:** She's after winning some oul award for entrepreneurship, Earnest and Something. Ah, she was lucky.

- **The Overstated Voice:** SPEECHES?! DON'TBETALKINGTOME! HALF-TEN BEFORE WE GOT THE MEAL. I WAS NEARLY DEAD WITH THE HUNGER.

There are also collective nouns that are only applicable to Mammies.

· **A good scattering of Mammies**: The group of Mammies that turned up to a function. This is especially applicable where there was a doubt about whether the function would go ahead.

· **A fleece of Mammies**: A group of Mammies going for a walk on the side of an extremely busy road.

· **A caution of Mammies**: Mammies on a school tour.

· **A pride of Mammies**: At a graduation.

Body Language

'I shouldn't have to say it to you. You should know.'

Irish Mammies will also employ physicality in conjunction with statements to give them greater emphasis. The *chin clench* is chosen where Mammy needs to express rage in a very controlled way.

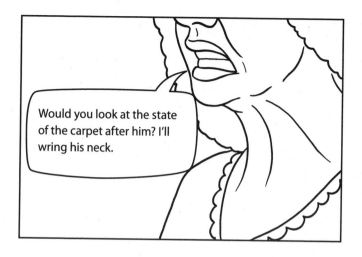

Similar in shape to the chin clench but with a very different intent is the *downturned mouth*. Its role is to convey Mammy's surprise at a turn of events in certain circumstances. For example, where someone she had considered a bit wild ends up exceeding expectations.

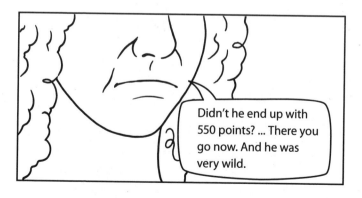

Bionic Mammy

'And they expect you to do EVERYTHING for them.'

As Irish Mammies evolved they also developed some new physical attributes that are verging on superpowers. These superpowers have never been celebrated in the format of a comic. Until now. Exclusive to this book are the cover and first pages of the latest superheroine – Bionic Mammy.

Soft Spots

There is a danger with all this iconicizing of Mammy that we forget that she is human. There are times when her thoughts stray to 'Someone Else'. Someone who she's always had a thing for. Here are some soft spots a Mammy might have.

Leonard Cohen

Leonard Cohen evokes something important for Irish Mammies: a past. He sings about quare carry-on in hotels in Manhattan, gypsy boys and an order of nuns who non-judgementally take in troubadours. (Especially troubadours who've been up to quare carry-on in Manhattan hotels.)

While Mammy may not have tiptoed across a foyer on the Lower West Side, she may once have done a steady line with an unsuitable arty-type who knew Phil Lynott. Or she had a fling with a cousin of Himself before Himself was on the scene. Now she listens to Leonard and her mind opens a box of keepsakes and finds a tattered postcard from The Other Fella.

Gay Byrne

There was no one like Gay. He called himself Uncle Gaybo and no one could argue with the title.

Presenters who succeeded him never came close to having blood relations with the country. They were more like in-laws. It was the morning radio show where most Irish Mammies 'made ears' at him. Mammies referred to him as My Gaybo and wrote in to tell him things they wouldn't have whispered to their best friend for fear they'd be misunderstood. But Gaybo never misunderstood.

Kenny Rogers

Mammy has always been a fan of grand singers but this is a different type of grand singer. One of the inspirations, along with John Wayne, for every man who strode bow-legged around an Irish country town with a cowboy hat, for every fella who 'went the money' and got a proper pair of denims – denims, not jeans – that fitted. Kenny Rogers could wear denim socks and get away with it. He is a man's man. And a Mammy's man.

The characters he sings about have a flawed past. Kenny's man knows when he's beat, tips a hat to the rest of the rabble in the room, and drives off down the freeway in a battered old truck.

Jeremy Paxman

She shouldn't like him. Talk about impatient! You couldn't have Paxman around the place interrogating Mammy about why no two of her mugs were alike, 'putting it to her' that there was no real need for a hot-water bottle. But what if he was in her corner? Imagine him not taking no for an answer until he got to speak to someone from The Council about the illegal dumping behind the ditch that was ruining Mammy's walk. Imagine him reducing a TD to a quivering mess when asked what was delaying Mammy's medical card. His alpha-male power would be exciting. And if he's impatient, what of it?

Helen Mirren

Mammies like the way she's carried herself over the years. And even more since she played The Queen. As if that wasn't enough, she did something that would feature in any Irish Mammy's Top Five Fantasies: storm out of a building and tell a crowd of drummers to keep the noise down. All while dressed as the Queen. Many's the time Mammy has wished she could give a piece of her mind to a few around the area but you have to be careful now in case you get more abuse thrown at you, or even be sued for 'causing distress', or worse. Dame Helen was a reminder that a justifiably cross woman in a grand outfit can get a result.

These are but glimpses of the complex character of Irish Mammy. Later on we'll see her out and about but, just at the moment, that IS the time and there isn't a child in the house washed yet.

2

Rearing to Go

You were as CRANKY. I used to have to put you out in the porch until you calmed down.

This book would not even contemplate giving out parenting advice. Even if the advice were correct now, a subsequent 'study' would contradict it. Parents today, and especially Mammies, are being tied up in knots about what is The Right Thing To Do. Advice on TRTTD is generally published as part of research done by a group of experts, academics and people with opinions. Such people are collectively known as 'They'.

What They're Saying Now

- They're saying now that if you put ground-up broccoli dipped in vinegar in their ears it should reduce the chances of nits.

- What are you doing, Mammy? ... No, no, you're not supposed to do that any more. It causes low self-esteem in later life. Actually, I I was reading it in that book you got me.

- It makes it WORSE? And there I was rubbing yoghurt onto her knees for years. Shur you wouldn't know what to believe now.

- They've a name for it — I can't remember now exactly what it's called, 'something-kinesis'. It's in the Living bit of one of The Papers.

'They' say plenty all through childhood, but it's when school days begin that advice flows thick and fast.

Big School

'Ooooooh, they're SOOOOO CUUUUUUTE,' says Ireland. During the tail-end of August, when the Summer Rains finally end and the sun comes out, thousands of small children go to Big School for the first time. Photos of little cherubs — 'Aahh! In their little uniforms. Couldn't. You. Just. Eat. Them?' — appear on the front page of the papers. For the broody, the first-day-at-school report on The News can be a tipping point. The sight of a Lazytown schoolbag and Hello Kitty pencil case can cause some women to spontaneously conceive — without a man or test tube in sight. When a little boy wearing SpongeBob glasses and a tie-knot nearly as big as his head appears on screen, even the flintiest-hearted males have been known to check their own torsos to see where they might fit a womb in.

But primary school is also the time when Mammies' little projects are launched on to a larger stage, and with it comes the inevitable worry about 'how they are getting on'.

And ... are they like this at home?

Parent–teacher meetings in primary school are a relatively new concept. In the past, Mammies' involvement in school was limited to a few specific areas:

- Occasional appearances on small-scale school tours in order to beef up security. (This sight of Mammy in an official context was a memorable moment in many a child's formative years, especially if an increasingly irate Mammy had occasion to 'lose it' with one of the child's friends.)

- Issuing directives such as Statute Number 4.2 in the Mammy Lawbook, which states that the child's cold means they must be Kept In At Break Time For Fear They'd Get Bronchitis Or Something.

Now Mammies and, where applicable, Himselves have to 'be involved at every stage of their child's progress'. This is of course a good thing. But it does mean Mammies are informed explicitly of comparisons between their youngsters and other children. What's more, at the back of Mammy's mind now is the possibility of so many childhood conditions that used to be misdiagnosed as 'easily distracted', 'boldness' and 'lively'.

They are also finding out new things about their child: how the presence of nature boards, having to share with other children, new phenomena like 'indoor shoes', and finding uneaten lunches in the toilet bowl can spark behaviours that have been hitherto unseen. And these come to light during 'incidents' in school.

If Mammy attends the meeting on her own, she may be able to pass off some of the feedback with the catch-all 'Ah … Just. Like. His. Father.'

And when Himself does attend the meeting, the different parenting styles may emerge.

GAELSCOIL MHICHIL Ó MUIRCHEARTAIGH

Nótaí Cruinniú Tuismitheoirí agus Múinteoirí

Ainm	Pól Ó S.
Rang	Trí
Muinteoir	Ms Ó Cinneide

I gcoitinne, d'éirigh go maith linn sa chrinniú ach ní raibh a fhios ag athair Phóil go raibh sé ag freastal ar Gaelscoil – tar éis 5 bliana!

Níor rinne me a thuilleadh trácht air. Bhí sé soiléir go mbéadh 'words' ag Mamaí Phóil níos déanaí.

Translates as:

In general, the meeting went well but Paul's father didn't know he was attending a Gaelscoil. After 5 years!
I didn't make further mention of it. It was obvious Paul's Mammy was going to have 'words' about it later.

Mammy remembers the meeting vividly and she pours out the whole story to her friend Babs in a breathless account during Their Run.*

> '… You had the … parent-teacher meeting … didn't you Fiona …?'
>
> '… Indeed I did … The eejit …I was mortified …'
>
> '… Ah he's … a young lad …'
>
> '… Not … Paul … his father …'
>
> '… Oh what's … Brian after … doing? …'
>
> '… We're inside … in the meeting and everything's going fine … Paul is "lively" but shur we knew that … next thing… Brian says … how he's … out for a walk … with Paul …

---

* Whether it's training for the mini-marathon, following *Operation Transformation* or just Clearing The Head, the roads are alive with the sound of Mammies. Drivers, please take care rounding a corner on any secondary route in the countryside as you may find two or more Mammies on Their Walk or Their Run. With their hi-viz glinting in the sun or the headlights, a stick for cross dogs and arms swinging in arcs of 270 degrees or more, the nominal reason for being out and about is exercise. Overwhelmingly, though, it's a social occasion, where news, hopes and fears are recounted. It also provides an important safety valve for discussions about Himself. Himselves may also be out on the roads, but they won't talk about themselves at all beyond a brief reference. Matters will swiftly turn to whether the exercise companion has seen the match last night, and agreeing that yes, that team is some shower of wasters.

and … Paul points at the sky and says "*spéir*" … and Brian … says to the teacher … that he's very surprised … how good … Paul is at the Irish …'

'… But isn't it …?'

'… LOOKIT I know … The teacher … looks at me and … says to Brian … "But you know this IS a Gaelscoil?" …'

'… What did Brian … say to that? …'

'… Nothing … I wouldn't let him … I said of COURSE we do and … we're glad that … Paul's … doing so well … I was MORTIFIED … Djumember us last year … cramming for the interview? …'

'… 'Twas like ye were in … the Irish oral …'

'… Well Brian got … an earful from me in the car … It wasn't *as Gaeilge* … I can tell you …'

Meanwhile, Himself recounts it differently in a conversation after five-a-side.

'Any craic?'

'No, we had the parent–teacher meeting today …'

'Oh right?'

34

'Ah 'twas grand …'

'Did you see the match last night?'

'Feck's SAKE. A shower of WASTERS …'

Given the essential part she plays in education, it wouldn't be any harm if some of the reading materials for very young school children were a bit more … well, 'Irish Mammy'.

There Once Was a Mammy

'… and she looks at ME as if I was the Wicked Witch!'

The fairy tales that we all grew up with left an indelible mark on our consciousness, but their origins in medieval Europe mean that we struggle to identify with them. The lessons we learn from them are a far cry from the reality of Irish childhood. The women are portrayed as wicked stepmothers, sneaky enchantresses or demanding mothers-to-be looking for forbidden fruit in a sorcerer's garden. On the other side, they may be fairy godmothers who can sort everything out immediately without any consequences or effort. There is a need for a more realistic character. Here's how our favourite fairy tales might look.

I'll never set foot in that house again

ONCE *upon a time there were three bears, who lived together in a house of their own in a wood – a Baby Bear, a Mummy Bear and a Daddy Bear. Every day as usual, they made the porridge for their breakfast. Just like us humans, they were very scrupulous about how their porridge was made. Daddy Bear's was done in the porringer with salt, Mummy Bear's in the microwave, two minutes thirty seconds at 700W, and Baby Bear's was a cooled-down couple of spoonfuls of Mummy Bear's with a bit of petit filou. This particular morning, they poured it into their bowls and they walked out into the wood while the porridge was cooling, so that they would not burn their mouths by trying to eat it too soon.*

While they were gone, Daddy Bear's Irish Mammy arrived at the door. 'The state of the place,' she said, after she let herself in and she started doing a bit of tidying. 'And they left all that grand food to waste. Of course, it doesn't surprise me. She was the same about the wedding. Nothing was good enough for her.'

So Mammy threw out the porridge for the cat to eat and continued to tidy the house. When she was done, she was tired and lay down to have a little nap. While she was asleep, the bears came back and Mummy Bear was furious.

'Eamonn, this is the last straw. You'll have to

say something to her. She can't be coming in here unannounced.'

'Shhh, Julie. She'll hear you.'

'Eamonn. I am your wife. Sooner or later you're going to have to stand up to her.'

Irish Mammy woke up with a start as she saw the bears looking at her.

'I know where I'm not welcome,' said she. 'Well, ye can forget about babysitting.'

'Ah Mam, don't be like that,' said Daddy Bear. 'It's just if we had a bit of notice. Isn't that right, Julie?' Julie said nothing and Mammy was soon storming down the path with the three bears scurrying after her. And that was far from the end of it.

I KNEW I knew him from somewhere

There are other fairy tales that could do with a reboot. In Rumpelstiltskin, the queen has to rely on a messenger to guess the name of the imp who threatens to take her first-born child. An Irish Mammy would need no such help.

I'm trying to place you ... you're not one of the Sheehans ... they're both fair. You've a look of the Galligans about you .... There's four of them ... the eldest boy is training to be a solicitor, and you're no solicitor haha ... What was the youngest's name at all? OH, I HAVE YOU NOW!!! RUMPELSTILTSKIN!!!

Too young to be out on her own

Rapunzel's Mammy, far from being the agent of her child's misfortune, would be the wise head protecting her daughter from the entreaties of passing knights.

Early Learning Centred

Textbooks for the younger children could also do with Irish Mammification to start the next generation off on the right track. The following extracts are part of a submission to the Department of Education for future curricula.

A day at the beach is an opportunity to give a lesson in the evils of waste and how there are always others less fortunate.

'But we're always having jam', says Kevin.

'Don't mind your whingeing', says Mammy.

'There's earthquakes in the Philippines and you're giving out about jam?!'

Whinge   Earthquakes

'One of them cakes tasted off', says Kevin.

'I know', says Deirdre. 'But Mammy will go spare if you say anything. You know what she's like about wasting food.'

Spare   Guilt

Mammy might be making tea but she's not one bit happy.

Mammy is annoyed.

'WHO calls to a house in the middle of the NEWS? And they'll stay talking until ALL hours, I suppose.'

Any bit of consideration

But whatever resources are available, whatever advice is given out, certain inalienable truths are self-evident and will never change:

A child[*] will always need a vest until Mammy says otherwise. And the day a study comes out that says vests are bad is the day Mammies march on science laboratories with torches and pitchforks.

Interest in Vests

In the United States it is called a tank-top; in Australia, where surely they have no need of one, it is a singlet; but in this part of the world it is a vest. It represents the thin white line between order and chaos, between a clean bill of health and a snuffly nose.

The word 'vest' itself comes from the Ancient Greek βεσταιρν (*vestairon*) meaning 'to wear something just to be on the safe side'. Although the Greeks rarely caught colds or double pneumonia, they still regarded the *vestairon* as sacred. It featured in many of their Heroic stories. Before the Achilles' Heel there was Denocraxalon's Chest. Denocraxalon was a warrior of great strength. According to legend, when his mother was with child a neighbour warned her that she should always make sure her child wore

---

[*] Child here applies to all those aged 1 to 70.

a vest because he could get a chest infection. And so it was that every time Denocraxalon went out into battle she warned him to wear his vest, until one day she delivered this warning while the great warrior was addressing a group of his comrades. Such was the laughter and ridicule that he vowed never again to wear a vest because he was grand without it.

And so he did, but the very next day, as he prepared to do battle against the Persians, Denocraxalon felt very run-down and was advised to 'take it easy'. The Persians, all well attired in their vests, duly triumphed and laid waste to the Greek armies.

The vest was extremely significant in pagan times in Ireland. At the start of June there was a huge pre-Christian feast called the Divesta. It was a time of debauchery and licentious behaviour, as whole villages would gather together, cast off their vests and go around wearing only T-shirts and short trousers. When Christianity came to the country, early bishops were horrified at the spectacle and attempted to try and appropriate the feast to one more in keeping with the new doctrine. The beginning of June was a quiet time in the liturgical calendar so it was just turned into a bank holiday.

Shakespeare's lesser known sonnet Number 107, '*Shall I wear thee on a Summer's Day?*' also extolled the seemingly magical protective powers of a vest.

Shall I wear thee on a Summer's Day?
Thou art so useful and so sheltery:
You could get an awful cold in May,
And this Summer too was very blustery:
Sometimes it be warm enough when the sun doth shine,
And you'd think you had too many clothes;
And one's fellows without vests maketh one pine,
Whilst perspiration drippeth from your nose:
But as soon as you would be in the shade
Or when that oul East Wind blowest;
While others shiver in the cooling glade,
Then I would be glad of you, O Vest:

Whether up a mountain or on the stormy seas,
O Vest you keep me warm and safe from all disease.

The vest was also much lauded in Victorian society.

To not wear one was said to be indicative of a certain lack of moral fibre, as can be seen from this advertisement from that time.

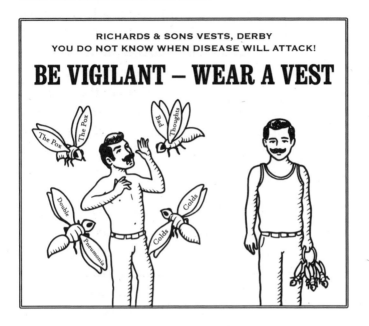

Hot and Bothered

Before we get too invested in pessimism, it's worth remembering that Irish Mammies sometimes have to deal with the occasional heatwave.

Mammies with smaller children are armed with Factor A Million to douse the flames of sunburn but she may have less control over older children and partners. Inevitably though, the White Irish follow the Irish Tanning Curve (ITC).

The ITC has a number of important points that are worth exploring in detail:

IRISH TANNING CURVE

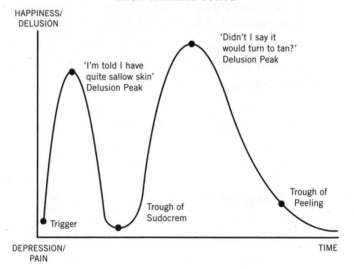

1. Trigger: A weather forecaster makes a statement like:

'Well after the last seven years of rain, it looks like the weather is settling down for a while and next week could see temperatures in the high teens.'

This sends the population into a temporary mania and there are ill-advised displays of often veiny flesh. With Mammy's warnings of sunburn falling on deaf ears, dependents gallop out the door protected by nothing more than sweat.

2. First Peak of Delusion: A person will experience amnesia about all their previous sunburn events and believe that they are, in fact, descended from a Spanish soldier who fought at the battle of Kinsale. The peak is marked by Mammy saying: 'You got a bit of a colour today!' but she says it a little sadly, knowing that to the best of her knowledge, the closest her family has ever got to Spanish blood was a rare steak Himself accidentally ordered on holiday.

3. Trough of Sudocrem: Yes, 'the colour' they 'got' was cerise. And the term 'bit of a colour' is sadly accurate, because the cerise is not uniform. There are a number of variations to the phenomenon of sporadic burning. If the victim was at a hurling match and stood behind one of the goals, depending on the orientation of the ground, they may be burnt on only one side of their face. Or there was a half-hearted attempt to apply sunscreen leaving white handprints on the skin, like the marks of a ghostly pervert.

The Trough of Sudocrem is where Mammy eventually steps in and advises action. It will usually involve at least one sleepless night where the sufferer is reminded constantly of their own stupidity, by the heat radiating off their own skin and the mixture of the smell of aftersun and burning flesh.

4. Second Peak of Delusion: In some cases, once the angry flames of the skin die down, the red may well turn to brown, leading the victim to conclude that they were right all along. They can tan. The tanner's self-esteem levels will rise hugely. They derive great pleasure from examining the white strip on their wrist where their watch was. The effect could be heightened by wearing a white shirt or blouse. Mammy says nothing. She knows what's coming.

5. Trough of Peeling: What goes up, must surely go down. The tan peels. It occurs – most heartbreakingly – at maximum brown-ness. Mammy will then helpfully remark: 'That's what happens alright.' And carefully place the suntan lotion within reach should the sun ever return.

For people with red hair, there are no such delusions. They can't risk it. For them the Irish Tanning Curve is very simple.

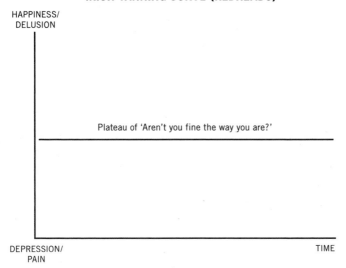

IRISH TANNING CURVE (REDHEADS)

HAPPINESS/
DELUSION

Plateau of 'Aren't you fine the way you are?'

DEPRESSION/
PAIN

TIME

But whatever they're wearing, or what the weather is doing, youngsters can't be wrapped up in cotton wool for ever. Sooner or later, they're going to become 'Active'.

3

Fierce Activity

They have to be constantly ENTERTAINED
these days.

B ored – it's a dirty word now. Bored children inevitably are going to Get Up To Something. That something will lead to another something. Before you know it the Squad Car is at the door inquiring about a series of scrap-metal thefts and asking why your child's *Busy At Maths* was found in a Grow-house.

Huge efforts, mileage and money are needed just to keep them occupied. The calendar on the back of the kitchen door is a riot of scribbled reminders.

Sun 1st	Petrol collection Father B Under 14 training
Mon 2nd	Taekwondo Ciara Pick up Prescription Order oil
Tues 3rd	Dentist himself Ballet Cathy
Weds 4th	Gospel choir PRACTICE Buns for fundraiser
Thur 5th	Flea collar for Sammy School tour last payment ZUMBA
Fri 6th	House insurance!!! Holy communion rehearsal
Sat 7th	FEIS!!!! Worming tablets for Puss

All of these outings take their toll on Mammies. Even getting their 'clients' out the door is a task. The advertising industry has unrealistic images of Mammies effortlessly filling a car with smiling, happy children, clutching the accoutrements of their 'activity' surrounded by the protective glow of L Casei Immunitas. The reality is they're already late because Child A can't find her hurley and Child B got the date wrong. 'Practice' was actually yesterday but that won't emerge until Mammy has driven the fifteen miles to the venue. Meanwhile Child C has just got sick on her car seat.

As well as traditional activities like sports, there are now speech and drama clubs, music lessons of various types, possibly even something involving a pony or a boat, Street dancing, hip-hop dancing, recitation, going in for *The Voice*, even computer coding if you don't mind. NO activity is off limits. Forget about Mammies wanting it all – children want it all.

Ballet-who?

There is no better example of this universal charge towards socializing than ballet. Ireland isn't traditionally a stronghold of the art form. The tights and general cavorting that went on in those godless Communist countries meant Junior B ballet training was never likely to be read out at the parish notices after Communion. But somewhere along the line it took root.

Originally, ballet was shown on RTÉ2 on a Sunday afternoon under the misleading title of 'Festival'. The programme started at two o'clock and finished at Never. It became synonymous with, and in fact came to resemble, a November afternoon: dark and miserable. Sometimes there was relief but usually in the form of equally grim, freezing-cold horse-racing from what appeared to be a moor. No one would stand for that level of Brontë-esque pall now but, back then, people just went through it stoically. Like the Extra Programme* — you just accepted that it was always going to be on and that was that. It was part of being bored.

When RTÉ got the money to buy other GAA games and the entire *Murder She Wrote* back catalogue, the ballet and the opera faded from sight. But it

---

*In decades gone by, before the concept of providing entertainment all the time became de rigueur, gaps in the schedule were common on RTÉ. Sometimes they were filled by the test card or action replays of AERTEL, sometimes they were filled by the Extra Programme. It was often a dystopic cartoon which contained powerful anti-authoritarian messages. Penned by a Czech man living a precarious existence just within the law, each frame etched meticulously by hand on the remnants of transparent refuse bags, the reels were smuggled out of the Eastern Bloc in the boot of a Trabant by a woman posing as an interpreter for an international symposium. They eventually made their way to Ireland, where they were watched by six-year-olds who were expecting *Tom and Jerry*.

is tempting to believe that it lodged somewhere in our psyches. The children of those who sat through the long, dark afternoons of the soul are all going to ballet.

On the one hand this is a welcome development — ballet enhances cardio, improves coordination and builds core strength, but it does leave a child poorly equipped for a party piece later on in life.

There will come a time at a country wedding when someone shouts out, '[insert name of ballet student] FOR A SONG'. This is not the place to trot out a half-remembered Dance of the Sugar Plum Fairy. It is therefore advisable to ensure that all children have knowledge of at least one ballad in order to participate in a singsong.[*]

---

*Singsongs: A singsong can erupt at any time — often egged on by Mammy. The key songs to know are ballads. Irish ballads have two basic forms:

- 19th century — Boy Meets Girl, Boy Falls in Love with Girl, Englishman Deports Boy to Australia

- 20th century — Boy Meets Other Boys behind Ditch, Black and Tans Arrive, Boys Hit Them a Few Slaps.

There are in fact so many ballads that, in many cases, the songs were written *before* the events spoken about took place, and it was left up to later generations to reconstruct the song. It was a common sight on lonely country roads to see a roguish gypsy, a flame-haired woman called Molly and an English captain with a purse of coins gathered together trying to play out the events of the song faithfully as they wondered what exactly a 'musha-ringdumadoodumadah' was.

Whatever the causes or result, the constant occupying means children 'have to be brought', forcing Mammies and Himselves to undertake a greater and greater number of Spins.

Rank in Order

With so much hithering and thithering to do, it is becoming increasingly hard for Mammies to keep track of where they are supposed to be at any given moment. Mammy's phone now resembles the radio base for a fleet of taxis:

> Base [muffled]: Anyone near the St Fluther's-Emmets-A-Ballagh pitch there?
>
> Car 1: I'm booked in to do that one but not till half four, Tony. What's the story?
>
> Base: Ref never turned up so the match is off. Can ya do it, Gary?
>
> Car 1: Ah, Jayzis, I've a million and one other jobs on but I'll try me best.
>
> Base: Sound man, Gaz. She's a good customer, been using us all her life, janoramean?
>
> Base: Steo, do you read me?

Car 2: Yeah, Tony, go 'head.

Base: We need someone around to Nana's. She's lost her hearing aid. She thinks it's down the back of the sofa. She doesn't need one but then she couldn't even hear me when I was trying to talk to her.

Car 2: Yeah, OK. Tell her I'll be there in ten. Just picking a child up off the ground. That OK?

Base: Good man, Beansy. Now any cars out there near Ballet?

Car 3: You're JOKING me. Not AGAIN!

Base: I know, yeah. Yer one who was supposed to collect her got held up again.

Car 3: 'Held up', me hoop. And she with all her money and nothing else to do. Held up watching *Shortland Street*, I'd say. I'm on me way.

Now, imagine if, instead of Tony, Gaz, Beansy and Steo and a fully functioning taxi base-control system, you have one Mammy and her phone. And of course ... The Car.

Mammy's Car

You can't do anything without a reliable car. Nothing fancy — just solid, like a pair of Ecco shoes.

This car won't be advertised with a man breaking free of the shackles of the urban landscape as he drives up into the mountains tossing his tie out the window. Nor will a group of annoying hipster friends race each other around the streets to find the quickest way from their pretentious house to their pretentious nightclub.

No, ads for Mammies' cars would be no nonsense, practical and tell it like it is.

IF YOU'RE NOT IN YOUR SEAT IN FIVE SECONDS, YOU'LL BE LEFT BEHIND!

The New Mammy 500

What's keeping you? Get in.

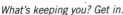

Following features as standard: Broken biscuits all over the car seat, a funny smell that no one's sure where it came from, the thing from the keyboard that was missing for ages. One size 4 Gola football boot, some socks from the U-14 team, a Nintendo DS game that cost a fortune and she must have only had it for a week when she lost it. Tissues, plasters, library books, scribbles on the back of Mammy's seat. Bodywork may be scraped but shur no harm done and what's the point in worrying about it with the car gone around the clock? Death-stares over the left shoulder at fighting siblings and TLC not included and must be supplied by driver.

Every day, Irish Mammies carry out seemingly impossible logistical feats without any plaudits. There should be plaudits. We should be packing the cinemas to stare open-mouthed at glowing red digital clocks as they count down and Mammy roaring at a child to LEAVE IT, WE DON'T HAVE TIME FOR THAT and IF I'VE TO COME BACK THERE, THERE'LL BE TROUBLE.

Moving Picture

The fast-moving caper doesn't always need guns, drugs and a missing bag of cash. A script about Mammies on a mission will do fine.

Gillian Foley

Let you look up to see where this Fleadh is on. You're a bit of a whizz at the computers.

Child

It's easy Mammy, you can do it on your phone.

Foley

Do it or there'll be no choc ices after.

(*looks at other Mammies*)

OK, ladies, here's the plan. You bring your own and the Quigley girls — I'll take my three, Mel's, and put the bodhráns in the back.

Caroline Martin

What about the harps? They won't all fit.

Foley

Of course they will.

(*Foley flashes a winning smile*)

Have I ever let you down before?

(*Montage with Cyndi Lauper's 'Girls Just Wanna Have Fun'. They arrive in time for the Fleadh and win a load of trophies. Foley looks at the pile of silverware*)

Foley

We're going to need a bigger car.

(*Mammies laugh, credits roll*)

For the most part, Mammies do the trucking with good grace. It's all about 'keeping them occupied'. But it takes hours and money to keep up all this activity. Small wonder, then, that every so often, Mammies explode in a protest so vehement it gives a whole new meaning to the phrase 'The Occupy Movement'.

And if the children are sporty, well, that's a whole other ball game.

4

It Keeps Them Out of Trouble Anyway

I can't watch it when they're out there. I say to Himself, just ring me after, tell me they didn't get injured and then give me the result.

Who's This He Is?

The range of Irish Mammies' attitudes to and involvement in sports can be summarized in the below 2x2 matrix.

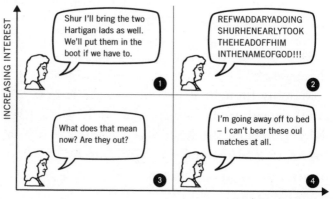

If Mammy is in Zone 3, a gulf may open up between her and her child. Picture the scene. A sitting room, with a curtain drawn to shield the television from the glare of the sun. The sport is rugby or soccer. Ireland are getting a tonking from some sophisticated foreign team with better-fitting shirts and a generally more urbane manner. The Child is scrunched up on the couch, their stomach a knot of tension and worry.

In another room, all through the match, Mammy has been hearing language that would curdle milk filtering through walls. She gathers that things are not going well.

Then, there is silence. It seems like the game is over. Mammy realizes that almost anything she says at this point will be the wrong thing. She takes a breath, goes into the room and says the wrong thing:

> 'Was it an important match? As long as they play well. I suppose.'

And she leaves again. She had contemplated raising the issue of The Language but decided to leave it.

Mammy thought it was all over. It is now. Yet another cultured Continental with good skin waltzes through the Irish defence to score a final insulting goal/try and the Child screams at the players, using an epithet for which the appropriate collective noun is 'shower'.

Mammy stops. The Benefit of the Doubt has now been rescinded.

> 'I don't care how many goals they've let in.
> I don't want to hear THAT WORD in this
> house again, doyouhearmenow?'

If Mammy is in Zone 4, she is more likely to feel the pain. Although she still doesn't want to hear That Word.

In Her Own Words

A lot of Mammies are in Zones 1 and 2. Across a variety of codes, the Sports Mammies are keeping the team going. They are rarely celebrated. Occasionally, one or two are thanked at All Ireland Winning Speeches:

> 'Finally, Three Cheers for a brave [insert name of county being patronized] team who gave us a good game today, a young team who'll be back again next year. I think that's it ... What? ... Oh Jeez, before I do that ... I nearly forgot ... thanks, Deirdre Fallon, for all the sandwiches after training ... [laughter].'

But most of the hours and miles Mammies put into coaching, transporting and consoling is unheralded. It doesn't appear in the closing *Sunday Game* montage. There is no book. Every autumn, the publishing industry prepares for the Christmas harvest. Like a farmer looking at the Long Range Weather, the book people scan the market skies for trends. What's going to be big this year? Hot Water Bottle-ology? Electric Blank-lit?

One genre has always proven to be a stalwart at the end of every year. It lines the shelves and stands of the bookshops in an impressive yield of tonnage per acre — it is the perfect Christmas gift for Himself: The Sports Biography.

The titles are strong evocations of the struggle the sportsperson has been through. Examples include: *Arse From My Elbow*, *Kicked in the Face*, *They'll Get It Across The Knuckles (If They Know What's Good For Them)*, *Back From The Brink But I Forgot To Get Milk* and *What Are You Looking At, Ya Bollox?*

Lean, chiselled faces stare out at the customer from the covers, their eyes a mixture of the hungry ferocity of the warrior and the empathy of the human being battling their own doubts and frailties. The hero is lit in harsh grey, standing in a post-apocalyptic wasteland, hurley/bicycle/kayak gripped to fight the demons of the universe — *but are the real demons in their own heads?*

All provide some insight into their minds:

> *The game against ComeAllYe Rovers was the big one. If we won it we would be four points clear with only two games left. It was do-or-die time.*
>
> *My routine was the same that day as every other one. I grabbed a protein shake and then had rice and chicken with the lads. No one said anything. Everyone knew it was the big one and it would go down to the wire, especially if as predicted, it became a game of two halves.*

The backroom team get a mention:

> Jonser was the best masseur in the business. When I did my ACL, he put me through hell, but it was worth it. I joked with him that if I'd let the missus do that to me I'd have been rightly screwed, but this was no time for joking.

But we rarely hear from the real backbone of sport throughout the country – The Mammies. Now it's time for that to change. Here we present exclusive extracts from the sporting autobiography of the decade – a warts and all account of life at the coalface of the GAA.

'Mammy, Mammy, we're going to be late for the match.' It's the second eldest. She's to be down at the pitch for a quarter to, and I can't find the keys high-nor-dry. Himself was supposed to bring her but he's out in the shed with the Boiler Man. Didn't the heating go last night? That's. All. We. Need. So now I've to bring Gráinne to some match. I'm not sure which competition it is. Probably the League, but I thought that was finished.

The Lord Save Us, it might as well be, the way they're going. They're getting beaten out the door. The poor cratur was in an awful state coming home the last day. 'We're useless Mammy. They keep picking Tracey, and she can't play at all.'

I. Don't. Say. A. Word. I know well it would be thrown back in my face. 'Well, why didn't you stay training them so?' is what they'd say to me, but shur I couldn't. I'd enough to be doing with the smallest lad starting school and twins on the way. But I'm telling you they weren't letting in five goals in a match against Oldtown when I was coaching them.

'MAMMY! We've to go now. I'll be late.'

I've found the keys. Where were they only inside in the youngest's coat pocket? The little DIVIL whenIgetmyhandsonhim!

We finally got to the match, and that's when the trouble started ...

The last line hints at the pain a Sports Mammy will experience, particularly at older age levels, when her child gets what is traditionally known as a Lambasting.

If things are not going well on the pitch, and the referee is not perceived to be giving them the rub of the green, some Mammies may take things a little too far.

The GAAAAH Match Officials Association

REFEREE'S REPORT

Date of game: 13.10.2013   Competition: *Junior C League*

Umpires: *M Cosgrove, P. Cosgrove*   Linesmen: *The two lads*

Teams: *Sharragee Bolshers*   vs   *Carricklough St Gobnait's*

Cautioned:

St. Gobnait's	Sharagee
F. Tierney B. Tierney	A. Whelan B. Whelan
S. Tierney D. Tierney (jr)	C. Whelan D. Whelan
F. Tierney R. Tierney	E. Whelan F. Whelan
PJ Casserley O. Littleton	V. Price T. O'Dwyer

Dismissed:
(Please cite rules)

D. Tierney (the uncle) Rule 132.1 "Retrieval of an implement from the side-line and subsequent use of said implement to assault an opposition teams Maor Uisce"

Remarks:

Following the final whistle a female member of the St Gobnait's supporters encroached on the pitch and proceeded to confront my officials and me. She made a number of allegations concerning my own performance. In particular, she took issue with decisions on incidents involving her son, who is one of the St Gobnait's players. I attempted to explain my decisions but she verbally abused myself and the umpires saying we were "as useful as tits on a bull". She also told me to "shag off back to Carlow if that was the craic with me".

Signed: *Gerry Cosgrove*   Date: *14.10.2013*

Mammy does the post-match analysis on her Walk:

'… I hear you … were … Man of the Match on Sunday …'

'… Oh Nuala … Poor Senan … had been kicked … up and down the pitch … for the whole game and … that oul eejit was doing nothing about it. I had to … give him a piece of my mind. I think … I was very fair in what I said.'

'… You were only … doing what … any mother … would do …'

Meanwhile, down the pub:

'How's Herself? Will she be taking over from Vincent Browne on the telly?'

'Ah feck off.'

'Gerry's isn't a bit happy. He's going around telling everyone he felt threatened.'

'I know. "I'm writing a report, Donie," says he.'

'Ah … his oul report. Tell him to shove it up his hole.'

'I could but I have to WORK for the fecker. And then She wants me to try and get him to rescind it. "Haven't you some influence with him?" says she. "He's YOUR cousin," says I.'

Great for the County Altogether

Not every day is like this. There are also the Big Days Out – in Croker.

There are two types of fans who make the trip. At one end of the spectrum are those who will 'Make A Weekend Of It'. Mammy on the other hand will be 'Home For *The Sunday Game*'.

The MAWOI lads start off their journey on the train on Saturday and limp home on Monday morning 'in tatters'. They triumphantly announce their presence on the train to Dublin with a simultaneous Qhuisssssh! as they open their first cans. They will bring a couple of apples for the journey. It's the only food they'll eat for 48 hours that is not cooked in vegetable oil.

On arrival, they'll have a few 'acclimatizers' in a pub in the city centre. A number of hours later they land – mowldy – at the apartment of their friend Barry who lives in Dundrum. Barry may express surprise at how lightly his friends have travelled. 'Where're the bags, lads?' Grinning, one of them produces a toothbrush and two contact lenses from the back pocket of his Jack Jones.

For others, a different weekend is unfolding. It's early on Sunday morning and the 'Home For *The Sunday Game*' Mammies and Himselves are herding a family of children, bundles of raincoats, flags and sandwiches on to one of the Special Trains laid on for the day. Himself is nodding and smiling, exchanging itcouldgoeitherways and dependsonwhichofthemwantsitmores with other passengers.

He's dressed in his comfortable trousers and a GAA polo shirt. Mammy's in a Windcheater. The Home For *The Sunday Game* man may shun the full replica outfit. It's not that he's a lukewarm fan, he's just not the type of man who 'goes in for logos'. He's the type of man who has a large bunch of keys and can procure so many tickets for big matches friends think he may be printing them himself.

For westerly and south-westerly counties, the final leg of the journey may be completed on a very packed Red Luas Line.* This brings the people of the country cheek by jowl with their urban cousins. Mammy remains expressionless as the family clearly hears a man resolve what she assumes to be a drugs-related logistical issue on his phone:

> 'Anto, Anto, listentome righ'. Anto, I swear, man. It's dere, righ'. It's in a brown bag, Penneys or sumpin, behind a bin near the railings, awrui man. Talkcha later man, bbbye ... Yiz up for the match Mrs? Aryiz goanawin?'

---

*The Luas is Dublin's tram system. Luas means 'speed' in Irish, although the term is used loosely. It's notable as being the first piece of rail actually laid down since the English left.

'Ah shur, we'll do our best, I s'pose.'

'Ah yea. Yiz can only do yizzer
best inanyways. Roi dis is me.
Bestaluckndamatch.'

As they watch him scamper off to his next rendezvous, Mammies will exchange good-natured pursed-lip expressions to indicate they all felt yer man was a *character* and no doubt off his head on something.

There may be a brief stop on the way to the stadium in a pub. During the week, the pub is a good deal saltier and was once on the news with Garda tape around it, but today there is diplomatic immunity for the visitors to the area. Mammy protects the children from the armfuls of plastic-glassed pints that are being passed over their heads while their father cranes his neck to hear what 'Spillane' or 'Cyrdil Farrdle' has to say on the small telly high up in the corner.

Every so often he pats his pocket and feels the comforting rectangular shape. They're still there — the tickets.

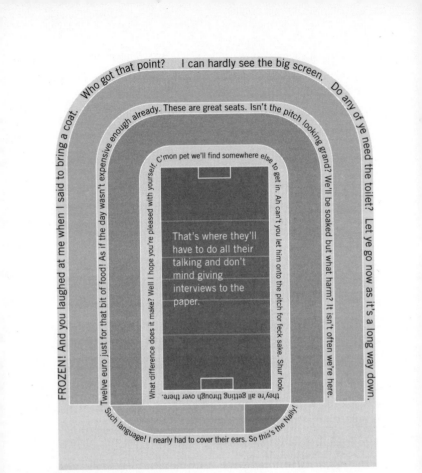

Terms and Conditions: This ticket is sold on the basis that you've some bit of interest in the game and are not just there because you got a free one from work and decided to go down to see what all the fuss was about.

The ticket is transferable especially to someone who was at the League matches and is a pure lunatic for going to matches or is the kind of fella that has a small radio (with no earphones) glued to his head during the match.

There's to be no blackguarding, flares or any of that kind of carry-on. We're not soccer.

5

Justice and the Peace

You'll get nice things when you start behaving
yourself.

The last book talked about the constitution of the house – on which the stability of the home is founded. That is but one arm of government. As well as the legislature, there is also the enforcement wing.

Policemammy

The Mammy PD is a formidable force and, apart from occasional waving of wooden spoons and, in certain circumstances, a flaking with a wet tea-towel, most of their weaponry is verbal. A complex array of defence-scrambling techniques can disrupt the most perfectly assembled excuses and arguments. Mammies are familiar with Sun Tzu's *The Art of War* and in particular the maxim that *supreme excellence consists in breaking the enemy's resistance without fighting*, or, to put it another way, 'I know what you're like.'

But Sun Tzu could never have imagined the array of weapons Mammies have developed and placed at their disposal. Here are six of the best.

The age card

'I'm surprised at you, at your age.'

This is employed in a number of situations – from a child thrashing about on the floor in SuperValu in response to the non-purchase of a metre of Fruit Pastilles, all the way up to a balding grown-up son making an eejit of himself doing the Full Monty in Cassidy's in order to attract the attention of Miss Macra. It's a devastating call to the child to look deep inside themselves and think about what they've done.

The race card

'Tisn't a race at all – you can go as soon as you're old enough.'

One of the great feats of Mammy sentences is the apparent use of two completely contradictory arguments to win the same battle. A tantrum thrown about not being let go to a disco can be a sign of immaturity. At the same time, the catalyst for that tantrum – being in a hurry to grow up – can also be stifled.

Rhetorical questioning

'What time do you call this?
Is that what you're going to be like today?
Who do you think you are, coming in here banging doors?'

All of these are unanswerable questions. Any child with a bit of cop on who is approaching an angry Mammy will have at least considered some possible outcomes and rehearsed one or two opening lines. Mammy's initial question is therefore designed to deflect the suspect from whatever excuse he has formulated. While the detainee is trying to come up with a reply, Mammy may then go on the attack by answering the question herself. She now leads 2–0.

Guilt

'I hope you're proud of yourself now! Ruining the whole day
for everyone. I blame myself in a way – I have ye spoilt.'

The child's behaviour is now not only a localized problem. It is threatening the very fabric of civilization. What's more, Mammy is now upset as well, and doubting her own abilities as a parent. Only the coldest-hearted of children would fail to respond in this situation. Below a certain age, this exchange will probably end with a conciliatory and heartfelt IDIDANMEANIHBAMMYI'BSLORRY.

Third-party insurance

'What would Nana say if she saw you behaving like this?'

Now the child has to consider his or her reputation in the eyes of someone else: someone who gives presents and brings sweets. The brand is under threat. Mammy is effectively threatening to go to *Liveline*.

The tissue sample

'Hold still will you!'

Sometimes, logic and mind games are dispensed with entirely. The key here is a show of strength so complete (yet without any implication of corporal punishment) that it can completely disarm a cranky child.

'WHAT ARE YOU DOING?'

'Nothing, Mammy.'

'Did you rip that?'

'I did-int.'

'And how in the name of God did you get your face so dirty? Messing, I suppose.'

'I was-int.'

'Ah, you're only showing off now in front of

[insert name of child's first crush].'

'I am-int.'

'C'mere till I wipe that face of yours.'

'NOOOOOOOOOOO.'

And then it comes out. Concealed in her sleeve, the tissue or hanky is deployed without warning. It is an instrument of humiliation that knocks the wind out of the windiest of sails.

It's probably just as well the late Venezuelan president Hugo Chavez never saw an Irish Mammy in action. He understood well the power of humiliation and used it to great effect. He would have brought political opponents on to his TV show, spat on a tissue and wiped them thoroughly around the mouth, accusing them of being stooges of the American imperialists and of stealing chocolate biscuits.

That, in theory, should be that. Mammy rules the house. Her word is unimpeachable – except, a new force threatens to disrupt things and suddenly Mammies' methods are being exposed for all to see.

There's One Going Viral

You don't need to tell Irish Mammies that viruses are an awful curse. If they're not hanging around wet coats on radiators or on the side of a half-eaten banana in a crèche, they are ready to pounce just before the holidays start.

But now there is a new virus in town – and this time, the pathogen is Mammy herself. Never mind your Gangnam Styles or your Harlem Shakes, the latest craze the ungrateful young whelps are up to now is filming Mammy in full flow.

Before, when Mammies gave out yards, teenage children sulked/sniggered/exchanged glances/said, 'OKAAAY, Mammy, I will,' but ultimately, most of them acquiesced. Now they slide the phones out of their pockets and without taking their eyes off them, press record and wait for Mammy to say something 'priceless'.

It's not clear what exactly is the precise motive for this. Perhaps they are seeking to become a 'social media celebrity' and imagine they will be granted their very own TV show where they review wacky clips from the Internet. Or they have seen how the Anglo Tapes made the news and wonder if they might be able to use it as leverage. Or they are just having what can loosely be termed 'the craic'. Or their perception of the boundaries between public and private is so blurred in an online world where every second button encourages you to 'Share', they may not realize the hydra they have unleashed.

The ubiquity of smartphones means that at some stage every Irish Mammy runs the risk of having her essence captured and uploaded. Forewarned is forearmed, and Mammies can reduce the worry such a privacy infringement might cause with the following tips.

1 An early warning system

Mammies could try to appeal to the better nature of their little angels, show themselves to be aware of the growing trend and deliver a shot across the bows in an attempt to prevent any secret filming.

2 Be the star

With or without threats, it's hard to get through to the Youth of Today, or indeed of any Day. Mammies should assume their offspring are gathering footage at this very moment. The child will think they are the hero, but the court of The Internet could judge the true champion to be Mammy, depending on what she says. In that case, Mammy should just be herself all the time but she should remember to throw in a few well-tested aphorisms to get the Internet on her side.

 Well done, Mammy – you tell him.

 Recording your Mammy when she was only trying to help. You should be ASHAMED OF YOURSELF.

 It's amazing. I earned nearly 400 dollars/day just from my own home. Click here for this unbelievable opportunity.

3 Take drastic action

If there is persistent recording by the child, then a lesson may have to be taught. In lieu of corporal punishment, the phone may need to be taken out of commission.

Treated Well

It's not all conflict. Like any benevolent dictator, Mammy has the power to distribute largesse and ensure the gratitude – for about 10 minutes anyway – of her subjects. The allocation and frequency of treats need to be carefully managed, lest Mammy find herself constantly on the re-treat.

Occasional treats are best and given as a reward for something, but there is little tolerance now for delayed gratification. Take the example of the poor benighted Coffee Creams. They didn't go with everyone's cup of tea but their stubborn presence in the bottom of the Roses or in a dark corner of the Milk Tray taught children a lesson that it's not always possible to have what you want. Then they were discontinued – a victim of the culture of Everything Must Be Amazing Now And All The Time. Despite this, the out-of-the-blue, once-in-a-while Mammy treat still wins hearts and minds.

A select few

Can there ever be a more wonderful object than a Selection Box? Yes it is true that on the 'Fierce Bad Value' scale it lies somewhere between 'pure cod' and 'a racket', exceeded only by an Easter Egg and sweets at the cinema. For Christmas, however, there is a brief cessation in the War on Bad Value and one Selection Box per child is put in the trolley.

While the artwork may look nothing special to an adult, for the child, the packaging is magical. The box has everything: reindeer, silhouetted conifer trees, snow on the front, a colouring competition on the back, Santa losing the run of himself hurling chocolate out of his sleigh. And then you open it and see all your favourite treats sitting in their own special moulded plastic capsules. The Curly Wurly, no longer slumped behind the Perspex in a noisy, surly city-centre supermarket looks even more attractive. It's like seeing your neighbours dressed up for a big local wedding.

Viennetta

As soon as it was first devised in Gloucester and those ads appeared, Viennetta was a special symbol of Mammy providing a treat. Unlike any ice-cream ever carefully measured out before, Viennetta was so luxurious and so rich, only a small amount would do you fine, or you would be up all night dealing with 'incidents'.

The ads were simple. Some sexy saxophone music played — not dissimilar to the scenes in *Dallas* where JR was about to make an eejit out of Sue Ellen once more, by carrying on with some 'secretary'. The Viennetta glided almost pornographically across the screen, its rippling surface reminiscent of the ribcage of a Venice Beach beefcake. As a silver ice-cream knife cut through it, there was an audible *plackkle*! And then a second noise as Ireland whimpered.

Naturally, a treat like this doesn't happen all the time, and when it is produced it is measured by Vernier Callipers to ensure that everyone gets the same amount in case there are any fights. You never forget the first day Viennetta arrived in the house.

Sweet stake

Ye Olde Sweete Shoppes have sprung up like Cash For Gold emporia in most towns around the country in the last few years. It's not hard to see why.

For bang-for-your-boiled-sugar-buck, it's hard to beat the sucky sweets — Barley Sugars, Glucose Fruits and Chocolate Oranges — and the chewy ones — Emeralds, Iced Caramels, Bonbons, Milky Moos and Scots Clan — that Mammy mysteriously produces on outings or from a hiding place in the cupboard. You can crunch or suck — it's up to you. There won't be another one until the following day. Unless you find the hiding place …

6

Life Skills

LOOKIT! Just get through the exams and you can do what you want afterwards.

They are familiar catchphrases: 'We're creating a nation of robots', 'Our education system is not fit for purpose' and, from our foreign multinational companies, 'Our students can't do maths.' Although, MNCs would do well to not moan about the country's weakness at maths. If we were any better at it we'd be able to understand how they manage to pay hardly any tax.

Underlying all of this is the feeling that education doesn't prepare children for real life, that it's just learning off useless facts by rote.

That may be true, but Mammy does not have time to ponder these conundrums. She can only prepare her children for the exams that are put in front of them. And if that means making sure they know their arsenic from their ox-bow lake, so be it.

First, get the qualification; then work out how to use it.

Of course, it's not all a grind. Many Mammies cut the children a bit of slack before the Big LC.

It's a Year Off, Is It?

'GET. UP. I won't call you again.'

Mammy's not in the mood for messing. At last count, she had a million things to do this morning and waiting for That Boy to get down that stairs makes it a million and one. Eventually she hears a stir, a series of clumps and then, some minutes later, a minor roll of thunder before the kitchen door opens.

> 'You're like a baby elephant coming down that stairs. Can't you, for once in your life try and … Wait a minute. What are you wearing at all and why are you not in your uniform?'

That Boy is dressed in hoodie, rude-boy trousers and … (is that eyeliner?) What kind of a—

> 'But Mammy I TOLD you, we're not in the class today. We're doing that flash mob.'

> 'Flash Mob?!'

Mammy's eye is twitching at this stage. 'The Flash Mob' – the very epitome of 'That's more of it'. She still worries about the time she caught him 'planking'.

'I told you loads of times. It's for Culture Studies, you know ... Transition Year?'

He holds his arms open in a I'M HOLDING UP A SIGN gesture that teenagers sometimes do when they're reiterating something SO OBVIOUS to their clearly dense parents.

Ah yes, Transition Year. Mammy has a few more names for it, one beginning with D and ending with OSS, but she holds her tongue. She let him go on it because all his friends were doing it and — she doesn't quite know how she fell for this one — because 'Mammy, I need some downtime after the pressure of the exams.'

'Downtime'. There'll be plenty of downtime on the dole, but again she bites her tongue. If truth be told, she actually doesn't mind giving him the year out to relax a bit. The young lad has definitely come out of his shell, and he was full of beans after the Anglo Criminal Trial Roleplay. What's troubling her more than anything else is having to listen to Kate Clancy going on about how Rachel is FLYING through Fifth Year and that they're already doing the exam papers. Mammy just doesn't want him to be left behind.

Maybe a delay mightn't be such a bad thing. There's no jobs out there anyway, so he won't miss much. It'll keep him in the country another year, and if he dosses a bit, so be it. The fun will be well and truly over once the Leaving Cert comes round.

I Can't Sit the Exam For You

❧

This is it. The Big Year. The tension ripples through the land of the Mammies. Nerves are frayed. Heads are nearly bitten off.

Six hundred years after it was first invented, the basic structure of the Leaving Cert has not changed. Many Mammies may not realize just how involved they are going to be in the whole thing, but by half-way through Sixth Year they will be completely immersed in the lingo and the speculation.

Cracking on

'Tis time now to knuckle down.'

This is an essential verb used by teachers and Mammies alike. It's hard for a child to define when they've sufficiently knuckled down, but they will at least have to make a gesture of giving up some sort of entertainment before the knuckling can be certified as being far enough down. Ironically, the phrase 'knuckle down' originated in the eighteenth century when it meant to start a game of marbles. But the Leaving Certs won't have any time for marbles, because they'll be too busy knuckling down.

Study aids

'You look a bit peaky. 'Twouldn't be any harm if we got you some sort of a tonic.'

There are two types of Leaving Cert supplement. Multivitamins and those advertised in the pullout supplements in the papers. The former can be taken with water; the latter with a grain of salt.

Exam Specials in the papers have a number of recognizable sections.

· The precocious child with the double-barrelled name who is writing an Exam Diary. The average Leaving Cert student finds it hard to identify with someone who has the time to write an Exam Diary.

· A celebrity reminiscing on their own Leaving Cert days. They will have very unhelpful anecdotes like 'I failed my Leaving Cert and now I am a multimillionaire. The Leaving Cert doesn't matter.' Don't let advice like that near your child. You haven't the money to be subsidizing that kind of Learning Curve.

- Tips and tricks from the experts. These are, by and large, sensible and appropriate, apart from one: 'Don't cram.' Anyone who has ever crammed for an exam knows they do all their best work at 5 a.m. that morning. The mind is focused like never before. The most important tip is never included — to wear a vest in case the Exam Hall is cold.

The Mocks

'You said that too before the Mocks and look where that got you.'

The sole purpose of the Mocks is to provide Mammy with proper leverage when motivating her slacking child in April and May. Any number of sentences may be begun that way.

- … now get off that oul Angry Birds before I put it into the toilet.

- … so NO, you won't be going on that 'Tweet-up Singles Weekend' or whatever it's called. 'Tweet-up' my eye.

- … and I think you've done enough 'de-stressing' now. Maybe if you were a little more stressed you might be better off.

Handy ones

'Why don't you do Classical Studies?
I heard Pat Taylor saying her eldest is doing it and he's
practically GUARANTEED an A.'

When it comes to subject choice, Mammies should beware the handy ones. These are subjects that have acquired a reputation for being easy.

In truth, handy ones are few and far between, but if you are a Bulgarian Mammy you need to be urging your children to do his or her native language. By all accounts it's a very телефон one.

The oral

'Look, I'll practise with you for the oral if you like.
Say it to me in French, what's your name? ... Right, and how
many brothers and sisters do you have? ... How many? ...
No, you've only two ... Oh you're right you've THREE! HAHA!
I was forgetting about Peter, thelordsaveus.'

The oral is a prepared statement given by the child to an examiner in a room in a language other than English. Regardless of the question asked, the child is trained only to give the answer he or she has learned off. It proves to be great preparation for any wannabe politicians.

The grind stone

'Julie Meehan's getting grinds?! What does SHE need them for? Well, if SHE's getting them, you'll have to get them.'

If the Leaving Cert is the Tour de France, grinds are the EPO. Practically everyone's getting them. They improve short-term performance but, long term, who knows what the benefits are?

Teachers

'Do ye still have That Teacher ... Whatshisname ... the fella you said was useless?'

There will always be one or two teachers on the roster who Mammy is worried about. This usually stems from them not 'covering the course'.

Before flying off the handle, Mammy should, for a while at least, consider the situation from the teacher's point of view. Perhaps they are fed up of ramming wads of education into unwilling young minds. Maybe they dreamed of a more unstructured education system. Instead of making pupils learn off by heart the five main causes of the Russian Revolution, they wanted to bring the class out for a day on the bog footing turf and teach them the names of the different heathers. Having said that, Mammies, when they've finished empathizing, would be advised to organize some grinds.

Time's up

'I met Geraldine Egan, in Supervalu, and even she says Kinsella is "coming up" this year. How she would know I don't know but still, it wouldn't be any harm to give him another read over.'

By the time June comes around, Mammies have become experts in all subjects. They nearly *could* sit the exam for you.

> 'Is everything ready for the morning now? Have you enough pens?'

One can never have enough pens and while you're at it …

<u>Exam Shopping List</u>

More Pens

Sucky Sweets

Lucozade

Rescue Remedy

Mass Card

Evolution of the Fierce Important Job

The point of all this hassle is to get into college, and the point of that is to get some sort of job so that you can afford the nicer things in life, like good tea-towels and scissors.

There is a school of thought that says that you should do what you love and the money will follow, but Mammies know this is not to be relied on – for a number of reasons:

· Love is fickle.

· Why don't you do something handy first and maybe you might learn to like it or at least you could love the money?

· One of the MacNamaras down the road is already doing what you love and has the whole thing sewn up. Her uncle - who is also doing what you love - is going to set her up with a job.

As the world evolves, so too will jobs that are regarded as Cushy Ones To Get Into. This is nothing new. Mammies have always kept a weather eye out for trends. They've had to. There has never been a sure thing that lasted for ever.

1900 Cushy

Dear Maire

Thank you for your letter — we are all well.

Albert is in the British Army, thanks be to God. He was lucky to get it. Isn't everyone they take.

And Brid, she's hoping to be a scullery maid in a 'Big House' somewhere and she'll be glad of it.. Shur what else would a girl be doing?

As for Frankie — or 'Proinsias' as he calls himself now. He has my heart broken. He got himself mixed up with a bad crowd — he's learning Irish. Irish!!!. What use is that going to be to him?

1975 Cushy

Dear Maire,

At last we have some good news.

Didn't Seamus get the call for the Civil Service?
He'll be set up for life now.

My knees were worn out praying for him. Isn't it a good job
now he got the 'A' in Irish?

2000 Cushy

STEPHEN GOT JOB WITH
THE PROPERTY
COMPANY GOOD MONEY
AND ID SAY PROSPECTS
R GOOD 2 HOPE YOU
ARE GOING EASY ON
THE DRINK

2013 Cushy

2050 Cushy

This is of course pure conjecture. The future has surprised us plenty of times in the past and will do so again, but Mammy's role as career advisor will never diminish. And why wouldn't it? Isn't she very well qualified — having done just about every role there is herself?

CV of Irish Mammy

Mission Statement

A mission statement, is it? I hardly have time to scratch, let alone think about a mission statement. I am up the walls with the small lad's earache and now Madam says she's bored with ballet and wants to do HIP-HOP. (I'll give her 'Hip-Hop'.) My mission statement now is to get out of here on time before some other thing goes wrong. Which reminds me, it's Mission Sunday.

Career History

Role:	Irish Mammy
Start Date:	Since The Day You Were Born
End Date:	Till My Dying Day
Role Description:	Oh, where do I start?

Skills

Project Management	Your father is a long-term project, but I'm managing him quite well at the moment. Haha.
Materials Handling	Another nosebleed?! Wait till I see if I've cotton wool.
Requirements and Needs Analysis	You don't NEED a biscuit at all. You only want one. They're two very different things.

Inventory Management	I will not. You've had plenty of Taytos all week. You'll be SICK.
Conflict Resolution	He did NOT get more than you. Your plate is bigger, that's all.
Negotiating Skills	I know, I know. It IS yocky but eat it up now for Mammy like a good girl.
Team Leading	Cmeretomelwanttotalktoyou … CMERETOME. Now, we're all going to have a nice time and we're all going to enjoy ourselves. And There's To Be No. Acting.Up. Do I make myself clear?

Education and Training

Oh, haha – there's no training for this. You just do it and hope for the best.

Interests and Hobbies

Well, after I've done all of the above and my own full-time job as well, there isn't much time for hobbies I can tell you.

Referees

You can ask anyone – I did my best and, if that wasn't good enough, well, tough luck, sunshine.

The Year in Review

You don't need to be a Mammy to know that the jobs market is precarious. Employers hold the whip hand, and they expect a lot from their new employees. This was easy to accept for those who were educated during one of Ireland's numerous recessions. They were just grateful to get any job at all and worried about 'work-life balance' later.

During the good times, expectations were raised. There was a rumour going around that you could be anything you wanted in life. As a result, everyone thought they were special. Even Irish Mammies forgot themselves for a while and let their tigerish defence of their children cloud their renowned common sense.

'How are you, peitín?'

'I'm fine, Mammy — not a bother.'

'And how's work? I was telling Mrs Twomey about your job, and she was all ears. "What's the high-flyer doing?" — High-flyer, she calls you.'

'It's alright, Mammy.'

'It must be nearly time now for your Annual Exam or Annual Review or whatever you call it.'

'I got it yesterday, Mammy.'

'And what mark did you get?'

'It's not a mark — it's an assessment. They give you this thing to fill out and you say how you did and they say how you did and then you are given a rating for the year.'

'Well, what assessment did you get?'

'I got a Below Peer.'

'BELOW PEER — what does that mean?'

'I don't want to talk about it, Mammy.'

'I can't imagine why you'd be below anyone. How many points was it you got, 560 or something?'

'MAMMY! I said I don't want to talk about it.'

But Mammy wanted to talk about it.

From: Mammy <paulinefitzmaurice47@eircom.net>
To: info@visionboxhorizontechireland.com

To whom it may concern,

My name is Pauline Fitzmaurice. Your employee Aoife – or
Aoiffe as she spells it – Fitzmaurice is my daughter. I was
talking to Aoife on the phone on Sunday as per usual and
she's after telling me about her Annual Review. Much to my
surprise, I learned that she got a 'Below Peer' mark. Now I
can tell you that Aoife is Anything But Below Peer. She has
always been a hardworking girl.
Did you know for example that she got 560 points in her
Leaving Cert, including an A-something in Maths? She
would have got more only for the way they marked the
English Paper 2.
Anyway, to cut a long story short, Aoife was very upset
when she told me about the mark you gave her. I can
assure you she is working fierce hard. Any time I ring her
she seems to be busy, so I would be grateful if you could
reconsider her 'rating' or whatever it's called and at least
give her the same as her peers. I'm sure there's plenty of
others in there not pulling their weight.

Yours faithfully,
Pauline Fitzmaurice

PS You needn't mention to her at all that I wrote to you.

For some Mammies, their children have had to fly
a little further from the nest.

7

They're All Gone Away

Himself says to me the other night — 'You'd miss them around the place, it's very quiet without them,' and he's a fella that'd normally LOVE the peace and quiet.

The children are making noise elsewhere now. But Mammy is listening out for any news. She reads about the Australian Gardaí being called to break up fights in Darwin, or leaks in the oil-sands of Alberta. She knows when hurricane season starts in the Atlantic and the different monsoons out East somewhere. She can do nothing about them. Neither, she suspects, can she convince them to get Mass. That's a lost cause. But, thanks to the Internet, she can enforce some element of control.

So Far and Yet So Near

In fact, it turns out Mammy can quite efficiently carry out remote discipline. For a start, there's Skype. You can't tell much from an email or a text, but you can tell a lot from Skype.

Not all children are as good at giving a ring home on the phone. They can pretend to be always 'out of the room' when Skype rings, to give them a chance to recover from a hangover/hide their tattoo/tidy the area of the room visible from Skype/get rid of the new 'friend' who stayed the night. Luckily for Mammy, this discretion doesn't extend to their online persona and they can't stop telling everyone else about their new life. Even if she 'had to find out about it on Facebook', a typical Mammy is now perfectly placed to join in the comments on the social networks and dispense a bit of long-distance tough love. And she can do so in the most effective way possible: in front of her child's friends.

The Eldest is after putting a photo up

 The Eldest Me, **Dee Flanagan** and **Ems (Ledgebag) Cassidy** on da rip n Sidney

 Mammy Would you not be better off giving your poor mother a ring and me with my two knees worn out praying for you besides to be "on da rip". AND WHO'S THAT LATCHICO BEHIND YE?

 Jonners hahaha! Nuals totes owned! Fair play, Mrs O!

 The Eldest Sorry Mammy – wil ring tmo.

Now Mammy knows exactly what they're up to. The scales have been lifted from her eyes.

 The Young Lad Dere'll b Sum craic on de 12 pubs tonite!!!!

 Mammy I thought you said you were going to go easy on the drink.

 DJ Gazprom Teehee wasting your time dere lady. This is gonna be off da hook!

 Mammy Is that yourself Proinsias? I hardly recognized you.

Children launching into diatribes on Twitter about a failing in modern society are reminded about the need for manners.

 Mammy @mammy   2s
@theyoungest You should be more careful what you say on this. You don't know who might be looking at it.
Expand

It's just as well for the child that there are still some tabs kept on them. Otherwise, if they ever have to move back in with Mammy, the adjustment might be too much to take.

Because, once they're back in the house, the old rules apply.

Home Again

'I mean, in our day, we might have had a few, but these days they just want to get OUT OF IT.'

The young lad stands outside composing himself. The taxi – with the muffled sound of a man phoning a late-night radio show saying 'I'm not bein' racist but' – has gone.

He was king of the taxi journey. Full of agreement with the driver, full of appreciation for the industry's struggles with The Regulator:

'Shur they've no understanding of your business.'

'This is it. You. Said. It.'

Now he's on different, shakier territory. Himself is out for the count, having wordlessly delegated the worry before he nodded off. But the son knows Mammy's sleep is on a hair-trigger. The slightest move could wake her and possibly lead to an uncomfortable whispered conversation about what kind of time he calls this.

He had breezed out the door earlier, humming a happy tune. Now his mind is playing tricks on him. The house that, during the day, was so familiar has become booby-trapped. He can't switch on too many lights for fear of waking the mythical creature upstairs in her lair – The Mammytaur.

So far, the mission proceeds smoothly. Even though his brain is compromised, it's not fatally so. He's remembered how the damp weather this time of year means the front door gets a bit stuck. He passes the cat, who regards him balefully, like a laconic doorman in a Manhattan condominium.

Later that day, Puss will attempt to convey the full story to Mammy in a series of mewls in an effort to get more chicken skin. For now, though, Puss will keep mum.

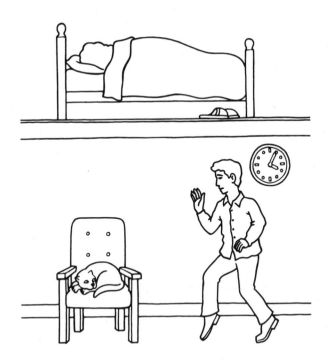

After briefly mulling over whether or not to eat fifteen slices of toast, the young lad decides instead to take the mission to the next level. The stairs is the final obstacle. Years of practice have taught him where the creaks are.

'*Is that you?*'

Not all the creaks, it seems. Either Mammy had pressure sensors put in when she got the carpet changed or one floorboard has mysteriously acquired a new creak. Light from under her door strides across the landing. She's awake.

'C'mere to me, I want to talk to you.'

This is not good. There is a huge difference in negotiating ability between a son who is a number of sheets to the wind and a Mammy who has been between the sheets worrying.

The combination of the darkness and the guilt gives the whole thing the air of a confessional. Should he kneel and say an act of contrition straight away?

The next five minutes of conversation will have to be conducted in a hoarse whisper so as not to wake his father, who might come up with some other questions. The key is not to give away too much. Too many words could get him into trouble and also reveal more and more of his breath.

'Well, were there many of ye out?'

'A handy enough crowd.'

The youngest reels off a list of the more sensible friends in his circle, leaving out some of the 'Legends' that could cause a narrowing of eyes and pursing of lips.

'I suppose you had a drink.'

This is always a tricky one. Mammy is from a generation when a few glasses nursed over the course of an evening should be enough for anyone.

How can he explain being out for six hours on

two pints?

Luckily, she doesn't pursue it. Like Tony Soprano's (lordamercyonhim) wife, Carmela, she doesn't want to ask any questions that would mean she knows something she can't unknow.

'There's a fierce smell of smoke off you. I hope you weren't smoking.'

Hmm – need to think fast. Going out in the smoking area just to hang around with the lads is not a good excuse.

'The taxi driver was smoking.'

'Oh, was he, indeed? I'm surprised he's allowed.'

Silence.

'Who else was out? Was WhatsHerName there?'

Mammy is fishing now. The youngest knows she thinks WhatsHerName is unsuitable because of a certain track record involving a fight Up The Town where the Guards Were Called. As a result he omits some details about where he spent an hour and a half between the chipper and the taxi.

'No. No sign of her.'

Mammy flinches a little in the dark as the lie lands on the carpet beside her. That wan was a pure rip.

She adds her — or rather her safe removal — to the Novena intentions list currently piling up in her frontal lobe.

> 'Well, off to bed with you and, remember, your father is going to the ten o'clock on account of the match.'

Groan — ten o'clock. Now that he's made a bad confession, he'll be doing his penance tomorrow. But given his current position, it's probably one Mass he'd better not miss.

8

The Second Collection

There were a good few at Mass I didn't recognize.

Mammy regards the packed church with mixed feelings. They'll be here for Christmas Mass alright, not knowing half the responses, letting the children run around. Still, it's nice to see them there and who could blame anyone for staying away? Although with a new fella in charge, who knows, they might be back?

Top of the Popes

'I'd say it got too much for him. Pity more of them didn't resign.'

You wait for ages for a new pope and two come along practically at once. It should at least be good news for the framing industry. Benedict was the first pope in a while not to be put up on thousands of Irish Mammies' sitting room walls. Irish Mammies, as a whole, drifted away from popes in the last decade. Benedict, for all his erudition, didn't sell himself well. And he lacked that all important pope attribute: the smile. The first John Paul had a grand smile. And of course John Paul II had a smile too, although Mammies' views on him are qualified. When he came to Ireland it was like twenty Oxegens without the carry-on. But there were a few things he said about women that ... well, Mammy would be too polite to say out loud what she made of it. This new fella seems to have a 'grand smile'. Some of the initial signs are promising, leading one to suspect he may have hired a few Irish Mammy advisors.

He even stays in a B&B and eats his supper with the lads. Mammy could put him up herself.

The honeymoon will end soon. At some stage he will have to make a speech, the basic message of which is 'Sorry, everyone, but those are the rules,' and this will lead to disappointment.

For the moment, though, he may just about make it on to Mammy's wall.

And no doubt he'll get an 'intention mention' at the event of the year.

Mass Appeal

It is early in Spring, shortly after the first official announcement of 'a bit of stretch' in the evenings'. A new warning is added to the usual suspects on AA Roadwatch:

> 'Raheen reoad is bumper to bumper …
> diversions in place … a truck has shed its
> load on the Farrybank dual carriagewaiy
> and there is up to foorty minutes of a delaiy
> in the area. Foinally, a remoinder that
> the Solemn Novena continues todaiy in
> Goolway, so you can expact delays on ool
> appreoches to the city throughout the daiy.'

There aren't tens of millions of Hindus looking for blessings from holy men who look like The Dubliners. Yet the Galway Novena is still a momentous occasion. No other event makes the AA Roadwatch nine days in a row.

Some of this is due to the fact that the Solemn Novena takes place in Galway – a city guarded by a Maginot Line of roundabouts designed to prevent a swift invasion of the city from the East by tank regiments. Yet, somehow, 130,000 people find their way through to get to 54 Masses and do some ferocious praying.

People who might struggle through a grand quick Mass in the local church are willing to sit in multiple ceremonies, because whatever it is that brought them there in the first place is a Big Deal.

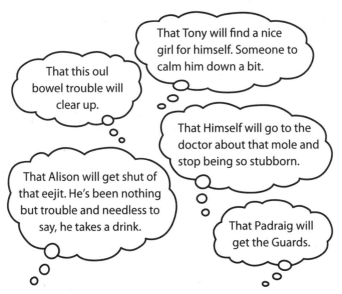

The Novena happens every year but there are the one-off occasions that can also fill stadiums.

Standing for Congress

The sky had a look of rain about it. A man with the name of his parish printed on a bib gathered up his wary charges at Connolly Station. With one eye out for 'gougers', the parish was going to the Eucharistic Congress.

As they got closer they were joined by other groups led by parish stalwarts in hi-vis vests. It was like the mustering for a battle in Narnia – without the centaurs and the half-men-half-bullocks.

A procession from Connolly Station made its way to Croke Park through some of Dublin's saltier areas, whose denizens rubbed their eyes at the sight of so many culchies. What puzzled them most was the *Live At 3* age group. 'Whatinthenaymajaysis kind of a match is on?' they said as the grey columns paraded past their windows, shod in sensible shoes, handbags clutched tightly for fear of running into Fellas Off Their Heads On Drugs.

But there was safety in numbers that day – like wildebeest parading past lions as they made their way to the ultimate watering hole for souls – the Eucharistic Congress in Croke Park.

Defying vertigo and dodgy hips, some Mammies climbed 400 feet into some of the eyries in Croke Park. And when they viewed the pitch it was like the revelation of some long-lost city. Priests and nuns as far as the eye can see. Joe Duffy and Mary Kennedy on the stage. This was Mass done by Cecil B. DeMille.

And on the journey home, they marvelled at logistics:

> 'They were sayin' on the radio there was 80,000 there. And we still got Communion faster than in our own place at home. Talk. About. A. Noperation.'

Another 20 Euro, I Suppose

There is a buzz in the crowd. They're waiting for the procession to begin. At the door of the church, the participants line up, ready to make their entrance. There are beeps and whirrs as cameras and iWhatsits are turned on. Hesitant dads are nudged by their wives to move around and get a better shot. The music starts and the boys and girls of Second Class troop in for their First Holy Communion Mass.

There is more restraint now than in the Celtic Tiger years. The Vegas days of the Holy Communion appear to be over. There are no tiaras threatening to be activated by remote control, no carriages waiting outside with golden livery. Helicopters are elsewhere, having been auctioned off by NAMA to Russian oligarchs and ex-NAMA staff.

It's left to the boys to rise to the occasion. Boys' Holy Communion fashion defies categorization. It has always been a heady mix of sensible and swanky, contemporary trends, expressions of parents' personalities and hand-me-downs. For every 'ah-isn't-he-grand-with-the-little-waistcoat' there is a primo don, gleaming in a white suit and Brilliantined hair. For every Denis Irwin there is a David Beckham. For every Henry Shefflin, a Paul Galvin.

Whatever the variation in garb, the children are all wearing big smiles. They're the centre of attention, and they know it. Older brothers and sisters must stew and hold their fire, unable to deploy sneaky pinches or flick ears. Younger siblings have been warned to behave; this is not THEIR day.

As Irish Mammy watches her grandchild go through the hand gestures of the Our Father, she wonders exactly how much of this is just a gesture from her to keep her happy. But she keeps quiet. Now is not the time to question the commitment to the doctrine of transubstantiation but a time to look on the bright side.

Anyway, Mammy can't be worrying about the ethereal or the next life all the time. She's got plenty to do with her own and, would you believe, even with the house emptying out, she's still busy?

9

Mammies at Large

I was afraid to stir out in this cold — but I. WAS.
FED. UP looking out at the rain.

Strangers on the Train

Whereas the bus into town has much the same cast of characters, just like a soap opera, the train is a major motion picture.

At some stage, an enlightened transport designer decided to put tables and facing seats in the carriages. For some, this decision has resulted in some uncomfortable hours avoiding the gaze of the 'odd' person opposite them. Every so often they sneak a glance at their travelling companion to top up their initial judgement, watching in horror as they peer obsessively inside a tattered Lidl bag. But when two Irish Mammies end up sitting across from each other, it's the beginning of a beautiful (but short) friendship.

Getting Started

'I don't know HOW we got talking.'

The newspaper

'Are you still reading that paper?'

'No, not at all, go on ahead. There isn't much in it godknows.'

'Deedn' there isn't but I'd always get it just to see the deaths.'

'It's awful about what they did to that poor man, isn't it?'

'Awful, Awful altogether. These gurriers ... I don't know ... They don't care, do they?'

'No. And it's the stuff they do be on. They're not in their right mind at all.'

'Shur this is it.'

The train itself

More than half a decade after their first appearance, the new trains, with their train-hosts and futuristic toilets that speak to you when you're at your most vulnerable, are still causing a stir. Though the new luxury comes at a price.

'These new trains are grand, aren't they?'

'But they're gone very dear.'

'Oh fierce — although, I've the Free Travel meself.'

'Goway — I wouldn't have thought it at all — you're very glamorous.'

'Oh now I don't know.'

'The Free Travel is great, isn't it?'

'I'd be lost without it — you know they can say what they like about Charlie Haughey but the Old People will never forget what he did with the Free Travel.'

The trolley

No matter how careful you are, no matter how well you think you've timed your trip to the toilet, at some stage, you will be stuck behind the tea trolley. You will peer around it like a driver trying to see around a herd of cows to wonder what gateway they might be headed for. You will sigh dramatically at every inconsiderate passenger who wants to see every sandwich available before he makes his choice.

'You were gone a long time.'

'Wasn't I stuck behind the tea trolley. There was a queue of us up there. We would have made AA Roadwatch! I was behind it on the way to the toilet and wasn't I behind it again on the way back?'

'Did the toilet say "thank you" when you locked the door?'

'I KNOW SHUR. Such a land as I got.'

This isn't the only opportunity the trolley presents to spark conversation — actually making use of it creates a little bit of drama. The tension mainly arises as Mammies wonder How Much Is This Going To Cost Them. There are price lists now, but buried in all Irish Mammies are folk memories of price shocks on the train in times past:

'And all it was was a teabag in a cup, a bit of a ... I don't know could you even call it a sandwich and I handed over the money ... A HUNDRED AND SIXTY POUNDS IT COST ME.'

Now that the prices in every other shop in the country have caught up with the tea trolley, there is almost relief when the young man at the helm announces the total.

'I thought it'd have been more, mind you.'

With this cloud passed, conversation will move on to Phase 2.

Fellow passengers

If neither toilets, train nor trolley have brought these two together, there is one last environmental variable — fellow passengers. Strangers have often kicked off conversations following an exchange of wry glances at the carry-on around them. It could be a cranky child, a group of stag-bound lads working their way through a churn of beer or overhearing one of the other Mammytypes on the train in mid-flow ...

Other Mammies in Training

Juicy phone call Mammy

This is a Mammy who has the rest of the carriage hanging on her every word. Shortly after the train pulls out of the station, her phone rings. You will recognize the ringtone, as it is likely to be the default one (unless a mischievous grandchild has had access to it, in which case Mammy is mortified every time 'Bad Romance' goes off in her handbag).

Once answered, it isn't long before her fellow passengers are ITCHING to know what the other person is saying:

> 'H— Hallo … oh, it's you … I'm on the train … Oh, stop the lights … A pure disaster … Ah they were all there of course … Yeah … and the solicitor … shur what could I do? … I'll kill him when I get home … I know … I told her she should have stayed away from him … Yeah … and the three of them living in the one house … And now Bernie tells me it's all on Facebook … What's the matter with them that they have to put everything on blooming Facebook? … I'll you tell you this much. There'll be no Florida now if I have my way …'

Researcher Mammy

A train trip can be very useful for Mammy to get
The Latest Information On The Young People.

'Where are ye going, girls?'

'We're going to a concert.'

'Oh. A concert. Isn't that lovely? And who's
playing in it?'

'One Direction.'

'One Direction. Are they a sort of a band?'

'Oh yeah. They're like a boyband.'

'A boyband — are they like Boyzone or do
they be singing their own songs?'

'I think their own songs but I'm not sure.'

'And where's the concert on now?'

'Down at the O2.'

'The O2. Is that the big place?'

'Yeah, it's big enough.'

'Aren't ye fine smart girls all the same
for finding yere way? Ye won't need any
directions to One Direction, haha.'

[nervous laughter]

Real-time-update Mammy

The new trains have another feature: the constant information on the train's progress.

> 'Hallo, it's Mammy. We're only 60 kilometres away now, so you might be thinking about leaving.'

> 'Hallo, it's Mammy. We're 30 kay away. Have you left yet? You HAVEN'T?! You could be stuck behind a lorry or a tractor on the road.'

> 'Hallo, it's Mammy. It's down to 15 now … Oh you're driving … I'll let you go so. You don't want to be getting any more penalty points.'

Meanwhile, elsewhere in the carriage …

Whatever spark is required to bring the two Mammies together, the asking of one key question should help take their relationship to a new level:

> 'Will there be someone meeting you at the station?'

> 'Oh, there will. My son will pick me up.'

> 'Ah, that's grand. Is he working above?'

And that's all that is needed. By the time the train reaches the destination, all manner of offspring accomplishments, flaws, aspirations, plans — including deeply held secret misgivings about offspring's new spouses have been aired. Consolation has been offered.

> 'Shur didn't you give them the best, what more can you do?'

The tannoy announces the imminence of their arrival.

> 'Arrived safe, thanksbetogod.'

> 'Yes indeed. Well, good luck now with your visit.'

> 'And you too.'

> 'Bye now.'

> 'Bye now.'

And they part, never to meet again, but the next time they get stuck behind a trolley or a computerized toilet thanks them for locking a door, they'll remember that day they Got Talking.

Salon Ranger

The train is one place where Mammy can let her guard down, relax, sit back and pour out her story; another is the local 'salong'.

Today, she's is getting a Do for a special occasion:

'I'm a bit early for you, Philip.'

'Not at all, Nora, you're grand. Will you have a cup of tea while you're waiting? Hayleigh, go and get Mrs Kelly a cup of tea there.'

(There's a Hayleigh in every salong. Sometimes ebullient but, at 15, she is often shy and awkward. She is far from her natural environment – slouching against a bus-shelter for 4 hours doing nothing apart from maybe scratching KT+HA+LI FRNDS4EVA on to the Perspex, thus obscuring an ad for 'A New Style of Banking'.

Where she is now is the hardest hanging around any teenager has to do – surrounded by relaxed Irish Mammies. She's the tensest person in the room – coiled around the broom, waiting for discarded perms to fall on the ground.)

'Hayleigh?!'

'But I'm still sweeping!'

'Go and get Mrs Kelly a cup of tea and a few … it's Custard Creams you have, isn't it, Nora? … a few Custard Creams.'

They both watch Hayleigh slouch off to the kitchen.

'Honestly, that girl!'

Philip starts speaking Irish Mammyish out of the side of his mouth.

'The sister is a bit worried about her, you know. She's a bit "wild". So she said to me would I TAKE HER ON. So I did and she's going around now with "a face" on her … And. To. Be. Quite. Honest. With You – I'd get more done without her. Anywaywe'llsay nomorehereshecomesnow.'

Philip breaks off as The Face arrives brandishing a cup of tea, followed immediately after by the rest of Hayleigh.

'There's your tea – jawant milk or sugar?'

The last question is barked. Philip makes a 'I think *someone's* in a bad mood' face.

Mammy is in heaven. A cup of tea. A copy of *Who's Let Herself Go*?! Magazine in front of her and a little bit of gossip about someone else's errant child.

Even if the niece was behaving herself, there would be plenty of guilty pleasure in listening to

Philip recount his travails with the some of his more deluded clients:

> '… But as I said to her, I'm a hairdresser not a magician.'

And:

> 'God forgive me, Mrs Kelly, but I had to tell her. "Bernie," says I, "for what you're asking me to do, you'd need a surgeon." Amn't I terrible?'

> 'Oh Philip, you are going to hell, haha.'

> 'If not for that, Mrs Kelly, then definitely for something else.'

At the same time, Mammy is also wary of what he might be saying about her, which is why she's always modest in her instructions:

> 'Anyway — what'll I do for you, Mrs Kelly?'

Mammy touches the back of her head.

> 'Just a tidy-up, Philip. Nothing too out of the ordinary. We'll be going up to Dublin tomorrow and it'd be a lot colder so I don't want to take too much off.'

> 'Dublin — isn't that lovely? This is for that thing on the telly, isn't it? Are you going on *XPosé*, showing them how it's done?'

Mammy has no doubt she could show them how it's done on *XPosé*, but her visit is slightly less glamorous.

> 'Haha, no – Tracey got us tickets for that oul Saturday-night show with your man, His Nibs. I only half-watch it myself, but I thought it might be a bit of an outing.'

> 'Indeed, Mrs Kelly, they should have you on it. You'd be a lot more interesting than them oul soap stars. I might even see you up there.'

> 'Oh, are you going up to Dublin, Philip? Just for a bit of a break is it?'

> 'Yeah, just treating myself for the weekend. I try to get up there now and again.'

Philip's mind briefly drifts to a certain type of pub in Dublin that he's sure Mammy has never been in. As she leafs through the latest edition of *Irish Mammy Magazine*, Mammy's mind drifts to a certain type of pub in Dublin that she's only DYING to have a look inside.

She'd already asked Tracey if she's ever bumped into Philip, but, says Tracey, 'What would I be doing on That Scene?' And Mammy says, 'I don't know, I thought you might have been curious to have a look.' But Tracey had made a face. She could be so small-minded, that girl.

Philip is snipping away at her now, so she has to keep an eye on him. Like most hairdressers, he has his own idea about Mammy's hair, and this has to be reined in by a woman who has asked for 'just a tidy' for her last 24 haircuts.

Some time later, after getting the roots touched up, half an hour underneath the dryer and a quick flick through an old copy of *True Stories of the Most Awful Murders!*, Mammy is done.

The Big Weekend arrives …

'Not long now, Mammy.'

'No indeed.'

Tracey and Mammy are sitting in the audience for *The Saturday Night Show* with a lot of other country folk. About five miles away in Town, Philip has met another man who's also in Dublin 'for a bit of a break'.

'Look, the camera is on you, Mammy.'

Mammy and Tracey look at themselves on the monitor in the studio. Or rather they look at themselves looking at themselves. This new angle allows Mammy a new view of her hair, and she gives a small exasperated sigh.

'That Philip. I knew he'd take too much off.'

Coincidentally, at that very moment, elsewhere in town, Philip is planning to do it again.

The Book Club

Himself eyes Mammy over his paper. She's muttering to the universe about 'how lucky it is that the very thing you'd need should go missing when you're in a hurry'. She riffles through some more bits-and-pieces and then pauses, before fixing Himself's general vicinity with a beady eye.

'Is it under you, I wonder?'

'Is what under me?'

'My book.'

'Which book?'

'The book for the Book Club.'

Oh, that yoke. Himself has never seen Mammy so stressed since she joined the feckin Book Club. There's a gang of them in it: Una, Mrs John Twomey, Nicola Dolan, the girl of the Fehillys, and a few others. The whole lot of them getting worked up about having the book finished on time. If they picked a smaller book to start off with …

'Well, GET UP, would you, till I see if it's under you.'

Himself sighs as he shifts on to one hip and sure

enough a 500-page paperback is retrieved. They are both slightly surprised such a substantial object could have been wedged unnoticed beneath his backside but Mammy hasn't time for contemplation.

Himself decides he'd better take an interest.

'How are you getting on with the Book Club?'

'Oh, don't be talking to me – I've only a few chapters read. I was hoping to get a bit more done but shur with Tess Clancy off sick I've had to do extra hours.'

The middle child arrives in.

'What's for dinner, Mammy?'

'Ye can fend for yerselves this evening. It's Book Club tonight. I'll be back around tennish, so behave yerselves now. Do you hear me? Ye've plenty of studying to be doing and stay off that oul Facebook.'

'I don't do Facebook any more since you joined it. I'm on Tumblr now.'

'Well, Tumblr or whatever you're on. Stay off it.'

The Book Club is a relatively new element in the social scene of a country that has to do much of its 'socializing' indoors. As well as the chat about the books themselves, there's the happy by-product of getting to see what the neighbours' houses look like.

Irish Mammies like a 'well-written' book — one with some bit of a story — although the modern penchant for stories that span many time periods and locations can leave Mammies, as well as everyone else, feeling a little drained.

A stunning epic spanning many centuries and locations, The Kite Thief's Pyjamas *is a high watermark in modern fiction. It tells the story of Ari, a young Baluchistani bronze worker who finds a strange message carved into an amulet. Thus begins a journey of discovery and wonder.*

This thing was an awful task altogether. Eight hundred pages. She had to give up halfway through. It was impossible to keep track of. Was the fella from the concentration camp the same one who turned up in Afghanistan? And what in the name of God was the ghost on the ship supposed to be doing?

The book before was a bit of work as well too. A book about 'Women' that they picked because Tess Cooney heard them talking about it on the radio.

I should have given Pat the comfortable chair on account of her hip.

I suppose poor Puss'll be wondering where I'm gone.

HOW did I forget that Noirín was a coeliac? No wonder she wouldn't have a scone.

... and according to Sheryl: 'Guilt management is as important as stress management.' What do ye make of that, girls?

Then there was the book that was a bit blue.

Mammy thought it was a great read herself, but then again she didn't have to read it out. Poor Selene Coyle – the poor Mammy who suggested it before she knew what it was about – the face on her and she describing all the carry-on. 'Oh girls,' says she, 'the things people get up to. It's a wonder anyone got any work done on that farm at all.'

The AI Man's Wife

'A SEMINAL WORK'
Times Literary Supplement

COLM O'REGAN

Whichever book they pick, the plot intrigues in it won't come near the ordeal of actually hosting the Book Club. Having the girls around to talk about books is all very well but they will be expecting to be fed and Lord knows what they'll make of this place and that oul couch. In particular Mammy is worried about Mrs O' – a lovely woman altogether but her place is an ABSOLUTE PALACE. The MONEY they must have spent on it. Mrs O' turned up at the last Book Club with her e-Reader. Cool as you like. 'It's the way to go now, Maire,' says she. 'You have to move with the times,' says she.

Mammy's not so sure. The times could do with slowing down a bit.

10

Put the Feet Up

Is there much in it this week?

A year after its groundbreaking first edition, *Irish Mammy Magazine* makes a welcome return to newstands. Following work with focus groups, it was decided to devote this issue to one subject.

IRISH MAMMY MAGAZINE

CUSTARD CREAM
Is this the King of Biscuits?

YOU WOULDN'T EVEN KNOW THEY WERE ALDI
Biscuits & Austerity

BISCUITIQUETTE
When to serve the nice ones

I ONLY HAD A FEW RICH TEA TO GIVE THEM
The pain of being Caught Out

Irish Mammy Magazine is also delighted to announce some exciting new regular features.

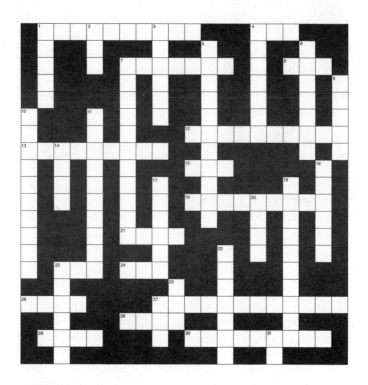

ACROSS

1   Remedial action in certain stressful situations. 'The only thing for it now is to _ _ _ _' (2,3,2,3)

4   Initials of the Holy Family. Usually invoked in other stressful situations (1,1,1)

7   Family pet whose indecision causes much annoyance (4,3)

8   See 26 across

12   Primary reason given for not being allowed to go somewhere. 'You've _ _ going to Oxegen. Don't I hear them on Joe Duffy going on about fellas who'd

be Off. Their. Heads?' (2,8)

13   Recommended reaction to misfortune especially if there's worse off than you (5,2,2)

15   A young woman of whom a dim view has been taken. 'The _! She has him led astray and he is too much of an eejit to see it' (3)

19   Previous location for a treasured object before a child moved it (4,5)

21   Boyfriend of ill-defined benefit. 'He's gone off to "find himself". If I "find" him I'll give him something to think about. How she got mixed up with that oul _ I'll never know' (4)

23, 24   Outfit for a wedding. I suppose we'll have to get a new _ _ for that (3,3)

26 and 2 down, 28 across, 14 down, 31 down, 8 across, 29 across, 23 down

        Indication that this new-fangled activity you are engaged in is at odds with your upbringing. 'Crosswords?! _ _ _ _ _ _ _ _' (4,3,4,4,2,3,4,6)

27   Term for Socializing where there is an implication that the regular allowance of said Socializing has been exceeded. 'You're going out again?! Haven't you enough _ for one week?' (12)

28,29   See 26 across

30   Most common reason for any disagreeable behaviour by any child under the age of eight. 'I'll tell you what's wrong with her now, she's _ _' (4,5)

DOWN

1   Along with horseplay, a common cause of mishaps. 'What are you doing with that chair? You'll break something, you're so _' (5)

2   See 26 across

3   Descriptive word for child who has passed acting-up stage and is now clearly bold, and possibly impudent. 'Well! You're as _!' (6)

4   Suggested reason why people may be laughing at child's grand anorak. 'Don't mind them, they're only _' (7)

5   Event that disrupts Mammy's rhythm completely. '*NATIONWIDE* IS ON?! But ... Oh shur today is Monday. This _ _ has me all confused' (4,7)

6   The marked absence of insects on the subject indicating he/she is unlikely to be feeble-minded. 'A Jesuit, no less? There'll be _ _ on him anyway' (2,5)

7   The reason for any Mammy decision where she doesn't have time to give a reason or there is no reason (5,3,3)

9   Hugely valuable commodity which may be in notably less plentiful supply than money (5)

10   Second most common reason for any disagreeable behaviour by any child under the age of twenty-eight (7,3)

11   A particular type of shame brought on by a child's behaviour, usually in front of other disapproving adults. Has religious connotations. 'When I saw the state of him coming down the church, bold as brass, it was _' (10)

14   See 26 across

16   Very. 'She's _ sure of herself for someone that hasn't done a tap of study' (6)

17   Sentence opener, usually preceding exasperation. '_ _ won't that one you have do you fine?' (4,2)

18   Mammy's hat at a wedding. She may have had 'awful trouble getting a _ to match the [23, 24 across]' (10)

20   Main reason for succeeding in getting a job in a depressed economy. 'Oh, he must have had _ because 'twasn't brains anyway' (4)

22   Third most common reason for any disagreeable behaviour by any child under the age of eighty. 'Shur what would you expect, he has them _' (7)

23   See 26 across

25   The other solution to all stressful situations if 1 across is not practicable (3)

27   A good one. Discovery of a mutual relation. Also funny. Similar to 'a scream'. 'That's _!' (3)

31   See 26 across

(For solutions see page 156)

Horoscopes

Aries 21 March – 19 April
Stoppit, Stoppit. STOP. Listen to me now, will you just relax and have a bit of patience? Honestly, you're as IMPULSIVE.

Taurus 20 April – 20 May
That's the good china now. You might be better off with a mug.

Gemini 21 May – 20 June
The pair of ye will have to sort it out among yerselves. Ye're old enough now to have a bit of sense.

Cancer 21 June – 22 July
What has you so crabby? Whatever it is, sort it out, because I don't want to be looking at that Face on you all day.

Leo 23 July – 22 August
You could do with a haircut. You don't want to be giving the wrong impression in the interview.

Virgo 23 August – 22 September
You're too picky altogether. You'll be left on the shelf if you're not careful.

Libra 23 September – 22 October
Which is it now? The Taytos or the Star Bar? You can't have both. C'mon! The ice-cream will be melting in the boot. Decide on one of them.

Scorpio 23 October – 21 November
Oh you're a sharp one and no mistake.

Sagittarius 22 November – 21 December
You'll have someone's eye out with that.

Capricorn 22 December – 19 January
Don't be a silly billy. You'll break it.

Aquarius 20 January – 18 February
That's a sign of rain. Shur bring the small umbrella. 'Tis no weight.

Pisces 19 February – 20 March
I don't CARE if you don't like the taste of it. Eat them up now and you'll be big and strong.

I suppose you have all the answers

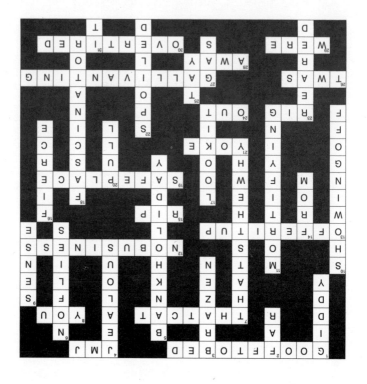

II

How Did We Do Without It?

Haha, oh indeed, I'm no whizz but, once you get used to it, 'tisn't that hard after all.

The first book of Irish Mammies recorded some of her struggles in a world where technology has seeped into every aspect of life. While *Isn't It Well for Ye?* may have been a work of unprecedented scholarship, its chronicles were incomplete. The relationship between Irish Mammies and technology is stronger and more nuanced than given credit for. A revolution has taken place with Mammies and the Internet.

Apart from the fact that they were always well able for it, there are a few reasons for this.

There's Better Gear Going Now

Having sacrificed decades to facilitating the gadgetry of their children, Mammies are now making up for lost time and bursting on to the World Wide Web through a gap in the world-wide ditch.

Mammy's introduction to computing used to sound like this:

'What's it doing now?'

'It's logging on.'

'It's very slow, isn't it? Way slower than the telly.'

'This is actually one of the faster ones.'

'And can I get On Line now?'

'No, Mammy. I've to dial up.'

'Dial up, I see. Where are you going now?'

'I've to disconnect the phone first.'

'DISCONNECT THE PHONE?! BUT WHAT IF SOMEONE IS TRYING TO RING?!!!!!'

(Some minutes later, following protracted negotiations about the phone.)

'Now click where it says "Internet".'

'"Click" …With what?'

'With the mouse. Remember I showed you how to use the mouse?'

'Oh, the mouse, yes. Ah, I'll never get the hang of it.'

Now, for a lot of Mammies, it sounds like this:

'Just touch that little button there with your finger.'

'This one. Oh yes.'

'And that one.'

'OK, wait now … Oh look, it's The Paper! Wait now till I see the headlines. "Minister Denies There Is Crisis In Health Service" … Isn't that great altogether? And what do you call this thing again?'

'A tablet.'

'A tablet — I wish all my tablets were as useful as this haha.'

And, once set up, she is away in a hack. Ever resourceful, like any new species in an unfamiliar environment (as long as there are no predators), Mammies are using the Internet in ways that more jaded generations would never have thought possible.

I Wasn't Born to Follow

Mammy peers out through the curtains.

'There's a car outside. Who's this now? ENGLISH NUMBERPLATES. Who do WE know with English numberplates?'

A young man emerges with a parcel. Mammy's suspicions are raised. A brief exposure to an episode of *Banged Up Abroad* has alerted her to young men and parcels. He approaches the front door.

Mammy goes to the door to investigate. Her children look at each other, wondering which Coen brothers-style situation their mother may be about to involve herself in.

From outside comes the conversation:

> 'Well, isn't that a good one? Honestly. Will you come in … oh … OK … well, tell her she's very good altogether.'

Mammy comes back in, still wearing her 'isn't that a good one' expression.

> 'Mammy, what was that all about?'

Her children are champing at the bit. When Mammy has a secret, it's a disturbing thing. Children are supposed to keep secrets from Mammy, not the other way around.

Mammy senses this and decides to play it for all it's worth:

> 'I bet ye're all wondering who that was.'

> 'Mammy, if you're getting involved in something …'

> 'Ah, would ye relax. Ye're worse for worrying than I am. That boy is a neighbour of Lavinia. My friend on Twitter. The girl who makes the grand porter cake in Cornwall.'

> 'TWITTER, Mammy! For God's sake.'

'Yes! Twitter. Aren't ye supposed to be the ones all up with the latest technology? Well, she put up a photo of the cake and I wrote a message to her saying that looks good enough to eat and where could I get one? I didn't say it all in one tweet of course, because they don't let you, so I had to spread it over a number of them — which if you ask me is a *pure cod*, but anyway, where was I?'

'You were making friends with strangers on Twitter, Mammy?'

'Now, yes, and so she said I'll send one of the cakes over but I was afraid it would get all broken so she said there's a neighbour's brother coming over and she'd give him the cake, and there you go now. Isn't it a small world, hah?'

'Mammy, this Twitter thing is getting out of hand. You're spending way too much time on it — and what about the Canadian?'

'Vernon?'

'Yeah, Vernon. Mammy, you spent 20 years telling us to mind ourselves with strangers and then you invite a Canadian fella you met on Twitter to stay in the house! What does Daddy make of all this carry-on?'

'Shur he doesn't mind a bit. Himself and

Vernon got on famously. We worked out that they might even be cousins.'

Down the road, another Mammy is meeting strangers too. Though not in person. She isn't sure if they would get on. They've already 'had words'.

The Games People Play

Two Mammies are meeting in a café for tea, a scone and a bit of oul chat. It's a familiar scene but this particular meeting will end in an impromptu lesson in - of all things - the 'App'. It starts conventionally enough:

'Well, how are they all at home?'

That should be that. The conversation should flow for ninety minutes, end with a good-natured row about paying and they would go their separate ways.

At some point, though, Mammy One spots a black rectangle peeping out of the other's handbag.

'Oh, is that the iPad? How are you getting on with it?'

'Oh stop, Dolores, THIS. Yoke. I think I'm after getting addicted to it.'

'Addicted — that's not like you.'

'It's this Words With Friends. Rose set it up for me on it. Says she, "Mammy, it would be good for your brain now to keep it active." Says I, "Worrying about you finding a husband gives my brain all the activity it needs." But I went along with it anyway, even though I HAVEN'T TIME for playing these apps.'

'Apps …'

'Oh Dolores, I don't even pretend to know what that is, Rose downloads this thing and says she, "C'mon, Mammy, it's like Scrabble. Do you remember you were good at that? We'll have a game. I'll go first." So that was grand, she went first. "Tree" or something she put in and she got 20 points for that. Then I had a go. It took a while to get the hang of it. You've to drag the tiles across, you see.'

Dolores is completely lost at this stage, wondering what dragging a tile means, and then she remembers she should get Himself to look at a cracked tile in the bathroom.

'And the next thing I'm playing games against all sorts of characters through The Internet. Gas isn't it?'

'Gas.'

Dolores feels a gap has opened up on the table between them. This must be the 'Digital Divide' she hears everyone on about.

> '…Tell me, Dolores, would you have any interest in it yourself?'

> 'Oh shur now, haha … I'm only just able to turn on the computer … haha.'

> 'But it's easy. Girleen, if I can get the hang of it, anyone can. Hang on now till I fire this thing up.'

She moves her seat around. They both Hold On A Second Till They Get Their Glasses.

> 'Now wait till I see, where is it? Oh yes … Words With Friends.'

> 'It's a grand nifty little yoke altogether. Where are the buttons?'

> 'You just touch the screen.'

> 'Oh, like the self-service checkout.'

> 'Now you're talking. Now, there we are. Oh, there's Himself wanting a game: OldStager65 is his name. Will we give him a run for his money? You've to try and make a word with these letters. Just drag the tile with your finger … No, you're letting it fall.'

Dolores's finger is not yet used to it — evolution

has designed her fingertips for checking a child's temperature, an aired pillow or a thousand other uses around work and home, but has not prepared her for dragging virtual letters across a window. But eventually the letter E is now positioned in the centre of the board.

'There you have it. Shur you're a natural.'

Twenty minutes later, the waitress comes over to see if they want more tea and finds two Mammies hunched over a glowing iPad, visibly excited.

'Benediction! AND A DOUBLE WORD SCORE – you're flying altogether, Kate. That'll shake up Mr OldStager, the divil.'

iMammy

Now that Mammies have taken to the tablets, the Apps industry needs to catch up and start making something useful for a change. Here are some initial designs to prompt them into action.

What's it like out?™

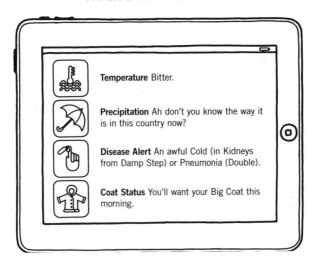

Temperature Bitter.

Precipitation Ah don't you know the way it is in this country now?

Disease Alert An awful Cold (in Kidneys from Damp Step) or Pneumonia (Double).

Coat Status You'll want your Big Coat this morning.

What's it like out? is an intuitive weather forecasting app that translates meteorological data into the most important updates any Mammy could need.

What is it you said you were doing?™

Another day, another Job Title. With every new permutation of the words 'Strategic', 'Quality', 'Delivery' and 'Manager' comes another profession for Mammy to have to explain to the neighbours. To cut through some of the fog, WIIYSYWD is a powerful communications tool. The child speaks his or her job description into the App and it will translate with a suitable shorthand so Mammy will know what to tell her sister.

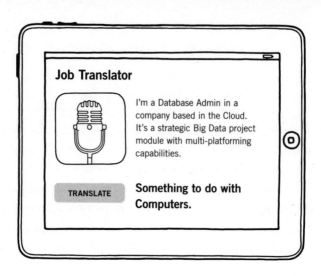

How are we for sliced pan?™

Exactly as it sounds — this is a lightweight and easy to use sliced-pan stocktaking system. It keeps track of how much sliced pan there is and reminds you when you need to get more.

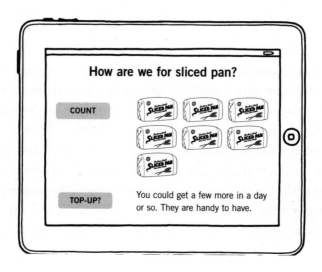

Email

Before we get carried away, it's worth remembering that not every Mammy can afford or wants to buy the latest in touch-screen technology. Some have found comfortable sanctuary at other little crossroads of the virtual parish. Not all of their life-affirming messages are sent to them via the Facebook walls of their pals. Perhaps spooked by stories of identity theft, cyber bullying, Twitter spats and whatever other horror stories of social networking filter through the prism of the media, many Mammies are perfectly satisfied with The Email.

Irish Mammies' inboxes can be a curious mix. Thankfully, they are spared the blandishments of Mrs Violetta Nkunge, the misfortunate widow of Former Ivory Coast General Thomas Edison Nkunge. These are sent straight to the spam folder – a location that many Irish Mammies have never looked inside anyway.

But they do get the fables, the messages, the stories of angels, prayers and gratefulness cards. Many are of the funny-story-with-a-message variety – like a *Reader's Digest* article about redemption in an unlikely place, the kindness of strangers or an unorthodox teacher. The emails travel the world, many times over, and arrive in Mammy's inbox having been selected and forwarded by a friend of a friend of a friend somewhere in Idaho or South Africa or Worcestershire.

The basic gist of most of these emails is that there are a few life lessons that some of the smart-arse, ungrateful, wasteful, complaining youth of today would do well to learn.

WEBMAIL

irishmammy@irishmammies.ie

| EMAIL | I DON'T | KNOW | WHAT | HALF OF | THESE | ARE FOR | Search |

FROM	SUBJECT
Idon'tknowHOWIknowhim	**FWD: A Lesson Worth Learning**
The Youngest	Re: Are you coming home this weekend or what?
The Eldest	Re: Did one of ye take away the phone charger?
The Sister	Nana's Will
The Cousin in Australia	Re: Are ye mixed up in these floods I see on the news?
Himself's Sister	FWD: MIRACLE CURE FOR CORNS
Sisters of the Blessed Hope	Your Donation
FellaIDidALineWithOneTime	How are you at all?

---------- Forwarded message ----------
From: Gerry Keogh < gkeogh1943@hotmail.com>
Sent: Mon 21 September 2013 11:45:15 +0000
Subject: FW: A Lesson Worth Learning
To: irishmammy (irishmammy@irishmammies.ie)

---------- Forwarded message ----------
From: LaShawne Benson
Sent: 21 September 2013 11:19
To: Daniel Timofte; Ban Ki Moon; FelixDaHouseCat; Stannis Baratheon; Moses Kiptanui; Gerry Keogh
Subject: FW: A Lesson Worth Learning

The teacher walked into the class. The students did not pay him any heed at first. These kids were tough. They did not give their attention easily. They figured respect had to be earned. The teacher went to his satchel and without saying a word began removing some vegetables and lined them up on his desk.

When he had finished, in a line on his desk, there was a tomato, an onion, a potato and a turnip.

Finally he spoke.

'Who can tell me what they are?'

'A FOOD LINE!' shouted Rafiq, who was one of the ringleaders in the class. His comrades sniggered.

'Very good,' replied the teacher. 'Who wants to eat one?'

'Yo, Teach! I will,' said another boy, the boy they called Tiny because he was the smallest in the class. He jumped up and grabbed a tomato.

The teacher smiled.

'Why did you pick that one?'

'Because the others would be gross.'

'Exactly. The tomato is the best of the foods because it has been above the earth in the sunshine. The others need to be cooked. Each one of you at this moment are like the onion, the turnip and the potato, because you are not ready to be accepted, because you have not turned towards the light of knowledge.'

Now it was the students' turn to be silent. The teacher said nothing more but, by the end of that semester, this class, which had previously flunked nearly every test, *became the highest achievers in the school*.

Because they knew they had learned a valuable lesson: when you are in the dark you are ignorant. They all learned to be tomatoes.

FORWARD THIS TO ANYONE YOU KNOW WHO IS A
TEACHER OR A GARDENER, BECAUSE THEY ARE
DOING A VERY SPECIAL JOB. THEY ARE GROWING
THINGS.

But it's not the youth that's concerning Mammy
now. With or without the Internet, as time goes
on, she'll be up to her ears in tablets. And getting
Himself to take them is a full-time job.

12

Get Well Sooner

I'd say I'm kept busier keeping your father
healthy than I ever was with ye.

For all the advantages afforded to them by history and culture, the males of our species still shuffle off this mortal coil earlier than (and often surrounded by) the females who had warned them to look after themselves. Especially in Ireland, where for generations men have regarded doctors with suspicion. When it comes to diagnosis, years of college and general practice are no match for an oul lad and his views on the universal restorative powers of salt, tea and The Bed.

Not that Mammy doesn't think there is some merit in this pathology, but she does like to consult the professionals from time to time. Her main challenge is getting Himself to do the same. And once he's in there, getting him to actually discuss any symptoms.

It depends on who you're talking to: 3

Consultation Notes	
Doctor's Name	The Man Doctor
Patient Name	Himself
Date	14/30/2033

Reason for Consultation:

Patient complains of feeling a small bit 'shook'.

Notes:

Patient does not report many symptoms, assures me that he's grand and it's just the wife overreacting.

Examined blood pressure   120/60

Prescribed notbadatol   2/day

Consultation Notes	
Doctor's Name	The Man Doctor
Patient Name	Himself
Date	14/30/2033

Reason for Consultation:

According to patient's wife, 'To tell the doctor what he should have told him yesterday.'

Notes:

Patient's wife explains that patient has had severe abdominal pain some days, has vomited and has complained of high temperatures.

Following examination of patient's abdomen, concluded he has a ruptured appendix and called an ambulance.

Discontinued course of Notbadatol.

Needless to say, this turn of events gets a run-out on Mammy's Walk:

> '... I mean ... in all fairness Susan ... imagine going in ... and not telling ... the doctor ... what's wrong with you ... He has ... my heart broke ... trying to look after him.'

> '... My lad ... is the same ...'

> '... "I don't ... want to be bothering ... people," says he ... Says I... "You'll be ... bothering a lot more ... if you get worse ... And if you carry on ... you won't ... be bothering anyone again ... because you'll be ... stone dead."'

> '... That shook him ... I'd say ...'

> '... I don't know ... whether it did or not ... He's above ... in the hospital now anyway ... Wasn't it a good job ... I packed his good pyjamas? ... Nora Reeve's nursing there ... Imagine her ... looking at Himself ... in his oul Italia 90 t-shirt ... and long johns ...'

Whereas Himself is again more circumspect about the whole thing.

Now that everything is back to normal, Mammy and Himself can focus on what's really important.

13

Who's Building That House?

Well, do you know how I found out? ...

The English left us many things — post boxes, a few railways that could be used for farmers' sheds, and arbitrary place-name translations that resulted in Trim, Clones, Tang, Tempo, Inch, Camp, Ovens and Pettigoe. But their most persistent legacy was an obsession with property.

Perhaps it's the knowledge that we're not getting any more of it and we didn't get to steal anyone else's; but acreage, road frontage, planning permission and extensions are what we fall back on when discussions about the weather dry up.

During the boom, it wasn't just young couples trying to put a foot on the ladder, or Celtic Tiger cubs with cuff-linky shirts, fellas who still 'hung arind with the-goys-from-skooel', or tough-as-nails pig farmers from the Border Counties who inherited the farm and then got carried away and built 600 houses. Mammies couldn't help themselves either.

Top five property-related Mammy sentences you'll never hear again

- 'They got 5 million for the field. Joe's going around with a ZERO-6. I'd say 'twas the first new car he ever bought.'

- 'Zoned, I heard.'

- 'It's supposed to be apartments.'

- 'Some sort of a hotel and luxury spa – if you don't mind. We'll all be going over to get our manicures, Breda.'

- 'It went for Big Money. A fella from Dublin.'

Top five property-related Mammy sentences you'll hear now

- 'The bank own that.'

- 'Or is it NAMA?'

- 'Whatever they were going to do with it, there's silage on it now.'

- 'It was supposed to be apartments but they say it'll be a school now.'

- 'I'm sorry I ever got involved in the thing.'

Some things will never change

- 'Where are they getting the money for that?'

- 'There was ructions over the will.'

- 'And. The. Place. Is. Only. Gorgeous.'

- 'They haven't spoken for years. Something to do with a hedge.'

- 'Have you met the new people?'

One other thing has changed. For years, the actual final sale price of a piece of property was a tantalizing piece of information available only to a privileged few, and even then no one could know for sure. Some neighbours underplayed amounts to avoid jealousy, others exaggerated in order 'to wind up Mrs Casserley. Don't you know the way she is with the questions. Eight million I told her. And I said you were buying a boat.'

All of that is over now, in a move which has revolutionized property-talk and gathered up the final tranche of offline Irish Mammies in one scoop.

> 'I'll tell you now how I found out Tara. I looked it up on DoubleU DoubleU DoubleU DOT Property Price Register dot I E.'

It's like the Golden Ticket to Willie Wonka's Chocolate Factory for Irish Mammies.

PROPERTY PRICE REGISTRATION WEBSITE
OR WHATEVER IT'S CALLED

SEARCH CRITERIA

ADDRESS
That house the Morans got from The Aunt, I heard it went for HUGE MONEY

COUNTY
When was it you said ▼

YEAR
You saw the Sale ▼

START MONTH
Agreed sign going up? ▼

END MONTH
Was it January? ▼

So powerful is this tool that it is practically core syllabus for Irish Mammies' computer classes around the country.

Though there is a downside to all this transparency.

Location Location Location

'For goodness' sake, close the door of that Hot Press. They'll be here. Any. Second. Now.'

Where there's money, there's talk and talk requires a venue. The valuation of every home in the country gave us a formal structure of something we've always craved. A class society. But first you had to work out which class you were in.

All around the country in the spring of 2013, gatherings were taking place. Neighbours shuffled into sitting rooms to have uncomfortable conversations with others on The Road about What To Put Down On The Property Tax Form.

(*BELL*)

'There's the door now. I'll go out and bring them in. Let you be boiling the kettle.'

'How's Paddy?'

'Not too bad. Is this where the summit is being held, hah?'

'Summit, hah? You're an awful man. Summit is right.'

(*BELL*)

'Who's this now at the door? Oh, 'tis Joe Mac and Maire. How are ye at all? C'mon in.'

'Ye've the place looking lovely.'

'Oh, well then, we'll have to do something about that. We don't want to be paying too much tax, hah?'

(*BELL*)

'You're a busy man, Frankie, 'tis like *Come Dine With Me*.'

Soon the neighbours are gathered. The tea is poured and it's time to talk about values.

There is a delicate balance. No one wants to pay too much but no one wants to think they live in a sink estate either. Plus, not everyone is there.

'No sign of the Fitzes I suppose.'

'No shur — they were the same about the neighbourhood watch. "EFF YE and YER NEIGHBOURHOOD WATCH," says Mrs Fitz to me.'

'They'll probably put up the value just to spite us.'

'Well, bad cess to them anyway.'

If 2012 was about *Fifty Shades of Grey*, this year is about nine shades of brown.

It's been a long day. Computer classes and property-tax meetings can take a lot out of a Mammy. Now it's time to flop down in her favourite chair, with one of the left-over buns, a cup of tea and a bit of telly. A tradition older than *The Hills* (or any other reality TV show), Mammies are very definite about what they like. Yet, a quiet revolution is taking place in what Mammy's watching and what she's watching it on. She has been left to her own devices.

14

Box Clever

How is it that we have 200 channels and there's even less on than when we had two?

For years, nothing changed. There were minor ripples like RTE2, 'multi-channel' and *Coronation Street* moving to TV3, but otherwise, life went on as normal. Then came 'The Saorview'. In theory this wasn't a revolutionary step but it was a wrench for Mammy. If there's nothing she hates more, it's throwing out a perfectly good set. The last of the solid lumpy TVs were reluctantly said goodbye to – the ones that never gave a bit of trouble. You could power them off a car battery and the rabbit-ears aerials made some sort of sense. Their respectable bulk meant you could put photo-frames on top of them and hide bills underneath. But they were unceremoniously carted off to the Recycling, to be replaced by flat tellies that seemed as if there was 'no stuff in them at all'. And for what? To have a dedicated news channel in case you missed the bad news. But Saorview got Mammies thinking about the television in a different way.

Once Mammies were freed from their loyalty to worthy old machines, a revolution started that this time around is not going to be televised. Saorview is being bypassed entirely. With their new gadgets, Mammies are watching On Line. They're on 4oD, The Player and The Netflix. Even for the TV itself, the guides have changed completely. From this:

	Morning	Afternoon	Evening	Night
TG4	**8am** NEWS?! At this hour?! Oh, *Euro News*. **11am** Leave it on there. Your father likes the Westerns.	**2pm** WIMBLEDON in Irish?! You'd still get the gist of it I suppose. **4pm** Tour de France in Irish?!	**6pm** Where do they get these weather girls from at all? **8pm** Leave it on there. Your father likes the Westerns.	**9pm** We really should watch this more often, but … **11pm** Doesn't Clint Eastwood look very young in that?
TV3	**9am** It's that morning thing whatever it's called. **12pm** Who are they?	**2pm** Will you take the money you foolish woman! Don't trust the Banker!! **5pm** She's gas isn't she, Judge Judy?	**6pm** We mustn't forget *Coronation Street*. **8pm** Turn On *Coronation Street*.	**9pm** What is that yoke? A reality thing is it? **11pm** I'd say Vincent will have a Face on him about this.
RTE 2	**9am** Cartoons I suppose. **11am** One of these Australian things. **12pm** Another one of these Australian things.	**2pm** Jessica Fletcher. Ah 'tis harmless enough. **4pm** It's all sport is it? I'll go out for my walk so.	**6pm** Is *Home And Away* still on the go? **8pm** The wildlife programme. Would you look at the leopard? Isn't he a divil for climbing trees?	**9pm** Is that a comedy? **10pm** This is the one they're all on about is it? Very violent.
RTE 1	**9am** It's that morning thing whatever it's called. **12pm** Is that *Shortland Street* or something?	**1pm** Turn on the news there and we'll get the weather. **3pm** Why did they get rid of *Live At 3*? Or even the thing with Marty?	**6pm** That was a quick Angelus you said. **6.01pm** Turn on *The News*. **7pm** Leave on *Nationwide*. **7.30pm** The Soaps. **8.30pm** The Cookery.	**9pm** TURN ON *THE NEWS*. **9.30pm** *Primetime*: It would depress you, wouldn't it?

To this:

THE 'HOW-DO-I-GET-THE-AERTEL-ON-THIS-THING? ...
WHICH-BUTTON ... OH-ISN'T-THAT-FIERCE-SNAZZY?' TV GUIDE

NEWS	THE SOAPS	AH, IT'S LIGHT	WELL MADE FILMS	WESTERNS
Grand Designs: Worst Self-Project-Managed Edition			Home Disasters	
Grand Designs: Ran Out Of Money Edition			Home Disasters +1	
Xtreme Come Dine With Me - Rainforest special			Eejit TV	
A Hoor For The Biting			Vampire TV Ireland	
Masterchef Armenia			Sky Caucasus	
The Great British Bake-off			Cake TV	
Celebrity Whist Drive: 45 To Save Lives			Sky Parish	

One Mammy is reported to have forgotten all about *Ear To The Ground* because she was stuck in Series 1 of *Revenge*. This is a new paradigm. TV used to be linear. You waited for something to come on. You watched it. You waited for next week. If you missed it, you regretted it. It was like life. Now it's On Demand. The choice has never been as wide. We do not know the effect this 'having it all' will have on Irish Mammies but, in the meantime, we might as well sit back and enjoy the shows. It's not clear if Mammies are hooked on *Game of Thrones*, *The Walking Dead* or *Mad Men* but, in the meantime, here are three blockbusting television series that will definitely catch their eye.

Game of Scones

From the makers of *Those Housewives Are Desperate Altogether* comes a labyrinthine saga that tracks the fortunes of a group of powerful matriarchs engaged in ferocious ructions.

Throughout the seven parishes, tension is spreading like damp. It was a short summer and now the winter seems to be going on FOR EVER. Do you know something? We're FED UP of this cold!
As the cold winds blow – will one of ye CLOSE OUT THAT DOOR?! – only a thin line of bravery separates the Rest Of Us from oblivion.

From *The Wall* where the young lads hang around, to over *Near The Shop*, trouble is afoot. Mammies are on the march getting a few bits in, sultanas and a pound of Stork. And all in fear of a tyrant of tender years.

Meanwhile in the far South, a new threat rises.

The Oven is hot enough. The players are ready. It's time for Game of Scones.

Dead to the World

In a world where nothing is the same any more, where mankind has lost its humanity, where life itself is a cruel joke, one Mammy tries to keep on keeping on.

'Tis All Oul Ads

It's the sexiest industry in the world – advertising. Madison Avenue, high-flying, fast-moving – it's all go. Everything is for sale and, remember: look good, look young, look relevant. *'Tis All Oul Ads* is the most stylish show to hit our screens and, in Nuala Draper, we have a formidable new character who will have you talking around the water cooler.

Did You SEE It …?

All the HBOs and Netflixes will never fully replace the communal TV experience. These are the programmes that Mammy and family still sit on the couch for and watch right to the end. Some of the perennial favourites are:

The Rose of Tralee

This is an opportunity to see 'fine solid sensible girls, grand and polite and no oul language out of them or anything. And look, he must be the escort. Isn't he a fine-lookin' fella too? Why did Daithi have to go asking her that? HE's a bit giddy. Whisht now they're announcing it …

'OOOOH … but which one was she? Ah, of course the girl who played the harp. She was nice too. Dubai, is it? And there's the mother. And a grand outfit she has. Very stylish. That must be the father. A YOUNG-looking man. That's it now for another year. It's harmless enough.'

The Eurovision

It shouldn't work, yet does. Maybe it's the tense anticipation of crazy Balkan or Finnish singers dressed as robots during a song about the Thirty

Years War. Or maybe it reminds us we are all part of a European family. (A family who for the last decade have snubbed Ireland in the voting, the hoors.) Nominally, Mammy is only interested in the voting, but she will look up from her paper at now and then during the three-hour show.

Anything royal

Regardless of their position on the national question, many Irish Mammies are fascinated by the Royals. We're starved of a bit of glamour here. Their aloofness is in contrast to the grubbiness of everyday politics.

Irish Mammies have a particular affinity for Yer Majesty because:

· She's great for her age.

· She has grand rig-outs for the big occasions.

· Her children sometimes disappoint her and her grandchildren can be a bit wild.

· Himself is a bit of a character.

The best thing about the Royals is that they are always on. Their slow-moving soap opera (with few mushy enough scenes) allows Mammy to project her own major life events onto a rather strange template.

Two years ago she watched William and Kate's wedding and empathized with guests who must have been waiting AGES for the dinner. This year, she watched the latest Royal arrive. Or rather she made great show of not watching:

> 'Can't they leave the poor girl alone. That child will arrive in its own good time.'

Until her curiosity got the better of her.

> 'Ah there's nothing on. Switch over to Sky there and see is there any sign of that baby.'

Finally, the wait was over and the weight was under.

'Eight Pounds Six Ounces 'Magine. YOU were Eight-Twelve. A fine big lump of a thing. I remember your Nana saying to me "Shur that child is half-reared." Oh! Is that them leaving the hospital? Isn't her dress grand? And a fine big jeep they have too.'

After that, only one detail remained.

'George, they named him. After the fella out of *The King's Speech*. No fear they'd have called him Diarmaid anyway.'

Mammies can't stay glued to the telly, though, because now, more than ever, their nation needs them.

15

Leading by Example

'Twould make you sick wouldn't it? I'd say I
could do a better job myself.

We used to have enough, for a few years we had plenty and now we have barely. Having experienced both extremes in one decade, it's time for a third way — one which balances prudence with positivity.

It's time for Mammynomics.

Mammynomics: The Basics

The problem with the Keyneses and the Stiglitzes of this world is their science is inexact and can be too abstract for many to understand. Any economy that obeys the simple laws of Mammynomics will be sound no matter what happens.

- **Fiscal prudence**: Mind your money, for goodness' sake.

- **Emphasis on quality**: There's no point in buying one of them cheap yokes. You'll pay more in the end.

- **Efficient utilization of existing resources:**

  - What's wrong with the one you have?

  - Every light on in the house and it the height of summer and OF COURSE the charger was plugged in.

- **Energy independence:** Don't be wasting petrol.

- **Robust bargaining in international treaties:** How MUCH?!

- **Limited targeted subsidies for SMEs:** To tell you the truth, I went in just to give him the bit of business. Shur he's very quiet in there, the poor divil.

- **Strategic investment:** Whatever you do, don't be arriving in there with one arm as long as the other.

There is a Better Way

The current crop of elected representatives cannot be relied upon to enforce the new ideology, which leads us to the inevitable conclusion: politics itself has to change.

A government of Mammies is a tantalizing prospect and they would be swept in on a landslide. The first stage in the business of governing would be the choice for Taoiseach, or Chairmammy, as the role would be called.

In conventional politics, plum jobs are often garnered by those with overweening ambition. The selection of the Irish Mammy Taoiseach would consist of repeated denials by all of the candidates until eventually a chorus of approval ushers the chosen one reluctantly into the job:

'You'll do it, will you, Pat?'

'Oh indeed, I will not. I've enough to be doing. Do you know who would make a great Taoiseach? Gráinne Scally.'

'OH STOP, WOULD YOU. HAHA! Imagine me now meeting the Queen in my oul duds. The very thought of it. Niamh Morley now, she's your girl. Fine and presentable.'

'NOW YOU'RE TALKING. Go on, Niamh. You're the woman for the job alright.'

'Oh. I don't know. I ...'

'And weren't you on *Nationwide* that time about the Tidy Towns? Talking away to Mary Kennedy like ye were great pals.'

'I suppose I was …'

'There you go now. I remember saying to Himself at the time, "She's a smart one that Niamh Morley."'

'Well, if no one else wants it …'

Once installed, the Chairmammy would have to assemble her cabinet. An Irish Mammy government presents an opportunity for true political reform.

The Committee

All home affairs would be run by The Committee – a formidable cadre of women drawn from ICA, the Tidy Towns Committees and one or two who regularly do the *Operation Transformation*. Within this group would be a Minister for Spins, a Minister for Minding Yourself and a Minister for There's A Lot Worse Off Than Us. Malingerers would not be tolerated and the Minister For Getting Up Off Your Backside Because No One's Going To Hand Anything To You On A Plate would be keeping an eye out for anyone not doing their fair share around the place.

In a new departure there would be two ministers for things Foreign. The Minister for International Relations and the Minister for Trade Missions.

It's all relative

The Mammy with the brief for International Relations would target as many world leaders as possible and work out whether they have relatives in Ireland. This was employed to very useful effect when Mammies in Moneygall noticed that Barack Obama 'reminded them of someone local' and began an unstoppable train of events.

Nun the wiser

The Minister for Trade Missions would be a veteran of decades of missions – the nun.

A woman who's made a life in jungle, desert, savannah and shanty town is the perfect choice for getting business done abroad. She knows no fear, having seen the worst already.

Culturally, she is tune with most countries.

And she knows where the opportunities are — forget about the BRICs. She's already built up an acronym of new trading links.

Tough talk

Finally, one minister is needed to take charge of all of Ireland's negotiations — the Minister For Being Fierce Persuasive Altogether. Only she has what it takes to join battle (over the phone, of course) with our most implacable European Mammy-figure: Angela Merkel.

We've already seen one Irish Mammy stand up to the Germans — Angela, the Kerrygold Mammy with the misfortune to have a son who thinks digging up a biscuit tin of soil is a good idea. When her German daughter-in-law passes a seemingly innocent remark, Angela tells her off: 'Oh shur we export all our best stuff.'

This kind of tough talking would prove useful in helping us in the times ahead as we try to get our financial deals from her namesake, Mrs Merkel.

'Hello? Is that Angela? This is Mammy.'

'Hello, Mammi. I thought it may be you.'

'C'meretomeIwanttotalktoyou. This bank capitalization thing, Angela.'

'Yes, Mammi, I'm listening.'

'Well, we can't pay it. By the end of the month we haven't a bob — maybe a bit for ice-cream — so I says to myself, "I'll ring Angela now and let her know the story."'

'Mammi, you have to pay — it was an agreement.'

'Well, I'm telling you, ould stock, we can't.'

'But, Mammi—'

'Listen, Angela, I'd better go now. *Coronation Street* is starting. I'll talk to you again. Bye bye. B–B–Bye Bye.'

And if that doesn't work, there's always the face-to-face approach, followed by distraction:

'You'll have tea, Angela, will you? Ah, you will. You're over here for the negotiations on the bank debt, are you? Milk and sugar? It's an awful state of affairs. I don't blame you for getting annoyed with that Anglo crowd. I was mortified when I heard the tapes. And they singing the national anthem. Wouldn't you love to wring their necks? And a bun? Ah you will? And you'll let the ESM take on the Banking Recapitalization? Shur you might as well. Ah you will. Sugar? No you don't strike me as a woman who takes sugar, haha. And you're happy enough with the corporation tax rate? Biscuit?'

And when she is finished saving the country billions it's time to start saving for Christmas.

16

Bringing It All Back Home

It begins earlier and earlier every year – the lordsaveus.

A Full House

'I suppose you'll be glad to have them all home.'

In medieval times, the first day of Christmas was Christmas Eve. Now, you run the risk of receiving a partridge in a pear tree much, much earlier. Every July, in a sequence aimed squarely at Irish Mammies, The News will present the annual report that Brown Thomas have opened their Christmas shop. The newsreader often pauses at the end, raising a quizzical eyebrow and practically egging Mammy to utter a tut-tut.

But you could hardly blame the retail industry. Consumers fed on nothing but bad news for five years are almost taking pride in how careful they are with their money. Why wouldn't the shopkeepers try to extend the season?

They can sale away. Christmas doesn't start until this arrives.

Christmas texts from an Irish Mammy, like all of her communications, are likely to crash your phone, such is the memory used up in processing their significance.

Whatever your return date for Christmas, it will likely not be early enough for Mammy. For Mammy, there is a satisfying sense of completion in getting all the children home in good time for Christmas. It's not unlike sorting all your CDs in alphabetical order and making sure all the discs are in the right box.

To avoid being the empty CD case, you change your plans. You miss out on the last party of the season—the one where romantic plans that had been bubbling away since September were finally about to come to fruition. Having made this sacrifice, you get home, anticipating a great welcome. And you get this.

After all that, your arrival is ignored as the house experiences a Mammy-led Christmas whirlwind.

Nevertheless, as a child of any age, the weeks before Christmas are without doubt the best of the year. It's better than Christmas Day itself and far better than the week after Christmas (a period of time known as the Coffee Cream of the Soul). Between the first stirrings of Christmas and the last desultory kick of the dying festivities, there are a few recognizable stages.

The Cards

The Irish Mammy Christmas-card exchange is what keeps the stationery world turning. Some cards have a leaf of Belvedere Bond paper stuck in the middle to pass on more sensitive pieces of information about bunions, gallstones and Himself's cholesterol. Others may be so perfunctory that it's not immediately obvious who the sender is:

> 'Wait till I see who this is from now …
> "Happy Christmas, Love to all … Una and
> family." Una, Una, Una … who's this now
> Una is …oh UNA!!! And she never sent us a
> card before. I'll have to look around now for
> one for her.'

But others with even less information are easier to decipher:

> 'This card is blank. It must be Mrs Foley.
> She's gone very forgetful.'

That's better than no card at all. The worry of unrequited postage plays on Mammy's mind:

> 'Wasn't it strange that she never sent one and
> she normally does? She mustn't be well. I
> must ask Mrs John Dooley the next time I
> see her. She has all the news.'

But if there is persistent offending, they are eventually struck off The List:

> 'Deedn' I won't bother sending them a card any more. Shur we never get one in return. He was never very friendly anyway. The father was the same.'

The Big Christmas Shop

The shackles are off. This is the fun shop. Messages are included, but joining them in the trolley are the mysterious ingredients for the cake, with their little shamrock brands. The ones the small boys and girls are really interested in are the Goodies: products with more Es in them than a bag of Scrabble Tiles.

> 'I suppose we'd better get the *RTÉ Guide*.'

As if there aren't enough landmarks to announce the holidays, the arrival of the *RTÉ Guide* surely marks the Rubicon. Even houses that buy it year-round get a special thrill when the bumper Christmas edition comes out around the 18th of December. Your whole holidays are mapped out in front of you. In the days of black-and-white television, it was the only time you could see certain people in colour and so finally solving the puzzle of Derek Davis's hair.

It's All Go

One clear indication that this is a special time of year is that doors are left open. Through the middle of an Irish Mammy-directed whirlwind, draughts wander freely like looters, aware that the normal rules have broken down. There is a cry:

> 'HOW DID I FORGET THE STUFFING –
> OF ALL THINGS?'

The Dinner

Christmas peaks around dinner. Mammy's at the centre of it: organizing, delegating, ordering unwrapped toys off the table and calling a halt to the pillaging of Selection Boxes:

> 'How many is that now? And you had your brother's Chomp as well. You won't have ROOM for your dinner – put them away this INSTANT.'

The good 'delph' is resurrected from the sideboard where it has been stored for the last 364 and a half days next to the deeds of the house and a phone bill from the Department of Posts and Telegraphs.

The new pope is talking, and for the first time people are intrigued to see what he says. The way he's been breaking with tradition recently he might sing 'Jingle Bells'. The children that are old enough are press-ganged into work, the rest on the floor — in the way.

And then it arrives — the bird. Lauded by the family but immediately deflected by Mammy:

> 'I-hope-it-isn't-too-dry.-Is-it-too-dry?-
> They're-so-sugaring-hard-to-keep-moist.-
> We-can-only-do-our-best.-Are-there-
> enough-potatoes?-There's-gravy-too.'

Woe betide any family member who isn't at the table on time.

> 'I WON'T TELL YOU AGAIN — SIT OVER
> NOW LET YE OR IT WILL BE GONE
> COLD.'

The family fall upon it like hyenas. Spuds disappear from the spuds bowl at an alarming rate but, as the scoffing slows, Mammy allows herself to relax for one moment until …

> 'Janey Mac, THE SPROUTS! I suppose
> there's no chance ye'll eat them now.'

All of this is watched closely by others who have kept their heart rate constant. As usual, they will be patiently waiting. Their time will come.

After dinner, the torpor sets in. In its heyday, even AERTEL took the day off. Given that it played such an important role, it was quite unsettling to switch on Page 100 to find HAPPY CHRISTMAS FROM AERTEL and nothing else. No mention of the stock prices on the ISEQ, the team news for the O'Byrne Cup. Just a screen depicting a snowy scene and a Santa Claus so pixellated it looked like he was being attacked by Pacman.

Thinking Outside the Box

By about 27 December, Mammy realizes the family can only consume so much and the surplus is distributed to others, whether they are in need or not:

> 'Take him up that box of Roses — we won't eat all of them at all.'

Roses are the gift that never stops giving. Cheaper and more numerous than Milk Tray, a box of Roses has always been a very acceptable way of 'taking the bare look off' your approach to a front door. Even if they were brought to your front door in the same way, don't feel bad; the recipient will do the same. The blue-and-rosey tin may make its way around the community — perhaps never to be opened. Like the wealthy merchant's 100 dollar bill in the parable of the village where everyone owes everyone 100 dollars, no one produced a box of Roses, no one earned a box of Roses, but the whole village had something to bring when they went visiting. In fact, this Christmas, why not scratch a tiny identifying mark on the box and see if it finds its way back?

What to Buy Mammy

- A nice scarf or something like that.

- A voucher — that'll be grand.

- That thing they were on about on the radio and didn't WhatsHerName do a bit on it on the telly as well. They're supposed to be very handy.

- That book, oh what's it called about the … ah you know the one … They're going to make it into a film.

What You Could Definitely Bring Mammy

'Mammy, we have some news.'

The Young Lad has become a man and finally given Mammy the prospect of a grandchild. Once the hugs have subsided, the reminiscing will begin. It is the ultimate bonding between Mammy and child-in-law.

In the initial announcement phase there are three main segments.

When are you due?

This is quite a short phase, as Mammy ponders the implications of a spring, summer, autumn or winter baby and reflects that, all things considered, any one of those times is a good time to be born.

> 'Ah Christmas/spring/summer/autumn, that'll be lovely.'

That would make it ...

This is a shorter unspoken phase, as Mammy involuntarily does a quick mental calculation as to the rough date of the start of the pregnancy, cross-checking it with any other information from that time – like, for example, the date of the wedding – and then moves swiftly on.

Oh, the trouble I had with this fella ...

Previously withheld nuggets about Mammy's own pregnancy and the Young Lad's early childhood will be taken out of the sideboard of her memory, dusted down and finally used again, like the good china.

There follow stories of morning sickness, hilarious infant behaviour and a lot of bodily functions, until the Young Lad who was previously a man has been repainted once again as a plump little bundle squatting helpless on the floor.

Himself briefly outlines his role

Himself will chip in with a description of heroic feats of pregnancy and parturition, including an account of his own inefficacy on the day:

> 'Talk about Women's Lib. Mammy drove herself into the hospital because I was in bed with the flu.'

The tea

> 'I'll. Never. Forget. The first cup of tea after you were born. 'Twas the nicest cup of tea I ever had and the nurses were saying the same to me. Of course there was no fathers in the delivery room that time. I suppose they thought they'd be in the way.'

Whatever your present, your presence is always welcome – although Mammy has had her fair share of callers this year.

17

Flying Visits

I suppose ye'll be anxious to head back now.

It had its critics. But most would admit, The Gathering made a difference to the country's image and self-image. About a year ago, Mammy Ireland sent the diaspora a text wondering if they had any plans to come home. Sure enough, they *did* have plans. 'Tx 4 invite. We'll b dere on Tues morn', they said. It was only then that Mammy Ireland realised, she wasn't ready for them at all.

Ireland has had its fair share of visitors over the years but they can be a double-edged sword. For centuries, they arrived *carrying* double-edged swords. Visitors now are far more beneficial but Mammy's sure they're going to notice things. Things like:

· Those cracks in the wall — what are they from?

· That hedge — it's gone very wild.

· The curtains — how did we let them get into that condition? They're manky!

And that's not even mentioning the ghost estates.

Undoubtedly, the best thing about The Gathering is that it has brought Family over from the States. The worst thing about The Gathering is that it has brought Family over from the States. Mammy was always tense when the Americans visited. Don't get her wrong; they're LOVELY people. What's preying on Mammy's mind is how she can possibly repay the welcome she received when she visited them a few years ago.

> 'Well, nothing was too much for them, SUCH A HOUSE. They even had spare toothbrushes laid out for us.'

For the lucky Irish family that had a chance to visit American cousins in the 1980s, the difference between the New World and the Old Sod was stark.

One couldn't but notice the effortlessness with which everyone was accommodated, the way the locals drank orange juice as if it was water, the size of the cuts of meat, the marked absence of any conversation about damp jumpers and airing bedding. Suddenly home felt like a few decades in the past. The memory of the contrast is still very fresh in Mammy's mind.

> 'I was there a week before I realised the place had a basement! Nearly as big as our whole house.'

As it happens, some of Irish Mammy's children have built houses 'nearly as big as you'd see in America'. But unfortunately those aren't the houses The Gatherers are interested in. They want to look at the small and poky 'Home Place' to remind them of where they came from. But Mammy needn't worry. The Irish-Americans — especially the nth-generations ones — are MAD about the place. They are enthralled by the thousand-year-old ruins casually scattered around the countryside:

> 'Hey Finbarr can I ask ya something? We passed this incredible, I guess you'd say, "Round Tower"? On the way here? I'm gonna look it up in the guide-book. What's it called?'

> 'Ah that thing has no name. Packie Furey uses it for storing bags of fertilizer.'

And once inside the house they are in raptures about the things we take for granted.

> 'Breda, your soda bread is just diviiine. I swear to God if you were in the States you'd have your own TV show.'

> 'I don't know about that now. 'Tis only the same recipe I've always used.'

> 'Listen to me honey, you're too modest! You're like the Martha Stewart of Counny Roscommon. And this jam, mmm-mmm! It's too good!'

> 'Well the jam is SuperValu.'

Emigrants who left a *Reeling In The Years* Ireland in the 1980s, who did very well for themselves in computers and by now have a slight Silicon Valley accent like the *Dragons' Den* fella, can be just as effusive. But they are used to logic, 'can-do' and constant improvement and every now and then they are reminded of some of the things that frustrated them about the country they left behind.

> 'Hey Mom, how come you don't get a new one? Make life a bit easier for ya, huh?'

> 'There isn't a bit at all wrong with it. It just takes a while to get going. You just have to be patient. There's a knack to it. As I always say, these things were sent to try us.'

The official Gathering did make one glaring omission. Hundreds of thousands of residents of Ireland weren't born here. We should have invited their relatives here too. It would have generated new revenue, taken some of the pressure off the native Mammies and also introduced Ireland to a whole new constituency.

And, speaking of the future, *Isn't It Well for Ye?* posited one vision of future Irish Mammies. But that is just one facet. What else will she be like, at all, at all?

18

What Will She Be Like?

You'll remember this when you have children of your own some day.

It is part of the cycle of life that eventually we will turn into our parents. Those who don't yet have children imagine they'll be the coolest, most rational, most 'with it' parents ever. We picture future conversations with our offspring, our voices reasoned and understanding, yet firm. But what will we be like in future generations? The messages will be the same, the dramas the same, though the environment will differ.

Well Wear

Have a look at *The Quiet Man* or indeed *Reeling In The Years*. What do you notice? The young women are dressed, by and large, like what we would regard today as Oul Wans. And the Irish Mammies of 100 years ago dressed like today's goths — with less eyeliner. The cycle is ever repeating. The Irish Mammies of 2050 will think of themselves as the most fashionable the world has ever seen. Children of 2050 will regard their Mammies with exasperation.

The Unusual Suspects

The prawn cocktail and the pavlova have become ubiquitous on menus aimed at Irish Mammy palates. But those who are now in the know would do well to wipe the smirk off their faces. In the future, they too will have their pet foods. No amount of eye-rolling by their own children will persuade them otherwise.

There will be a wedding in a half-century or so and the first sight of the menu will be greeted with 'ooh's and 'aah's by most of those present.

But in the corner will be someone's Mammy, pursing her lips at the vol-au-wasp and the test-tube-grown marmoset. She will spy a waiter floating by on his HoverSegway and raise her arm — against the protestations of her daughter.

> 'Is everything OK for you?'
>
> [*Daughter, in a fierce whisper*] 'Mam. Don't. Can't you eat what's there?'
>
> 'I'm only going to ask him. Shur if they don't have it, they can say it.' [*Turning to the waiter*] 'If it isn't too much trouble, could I ask you something?'
>
> 'Of course Madam, that's what we're here for.'
>
> 'By any chance would ye have a goat's cheese tartlet or a bit of a rocket and walnut and pear salad? I'm sorry now, you must think me fierce old-fashioned.'

The waiter is trained to deal with these situations.

> 'Not at all Madam, I'm sure we'll be able to rustle up something. So will I take away the cricket soup and the larvae fritters?'
>
> 'Well I'd hate to see it go to waste. Would anyone else eat it?'
>
> 'Oh 'twont go to waste at all.'
>
> [*Waiter goes*]

'Now, Mam, are you happy? Would you not try a bit of locust, you'd love it alright.'

'Look it, Cassiopeia — I know what I like, and that's that. That oul new stuff wouldn't agree with me at all. I'd be just as happy with a bit of couscous and feta. It was good enough for all of ye growing up.'

And speaking of weddings, throughout much of the world a debate rages about 'tradition' and what a marriage 'should be'. In decades to come, the norm will look very different.

The Parting Glass

In 2050, when Mammy looks fondly back at her own youth — misspent or otherwise — what will she be nostalgic about? The singsong will survive but in the intervening years, no new ballads will have been written. Maybe what is regarded as 'noise' now will be remembered with misty eyes in a generation's time.

And there we leave Mammy for the time being, lost in thought. One eye on the past, one on the future, and the eyes in the back of her head fixed firmly on us.

Acknowledgements

Thanks once again to Brian, Eoin and all at Transworld. Their advice and editing - especially during 'the difficult second album phase' when I insisted on 20-minute instrumentals - was measured and spot-on.

Thanks to Faith and all at the Lisa Richards Agency for their invaluable support and advice for helping me negotiate a whole new world of funny.

Thanks to Doug Ferris, who has brought more parts of the Irish Mammy universe to life with his excellent illustrations.

Many thanks to the great people at Curious Design for their patience while laying out a book with 100 illustrations as well as producing the diagrams.

For my wife Marie, I love you very much.

For my mother and father who have been a wonderful source of love and support throughout my life.

In the past year, the Twitter followers of Irish Mammy have doubled to more than 100,000. They are a humorous and friendly bunch whose own observations of theirs and their Mammies' behaviour has made this whole endeavour so enjoyable.

About the Author

Colm O'Regan is a critically acclaimed stand-up comedian, columnist and broadcaster.

He writes a weekly column for *The Irish Examiner* and has written for *The Irish Times* and *BBC Online Magazine*. Colm is a regular contributor on Irish radio and on the BBC World Service. As a stand-up comedian, he has performed to sell-out crowds all over the world from Tokyo to Cape Town and including the Edinburgh Fringe, the Cat Laughs and the Montreal Just For Laughs Festival. His stand-up has also featured on RTÉ's *Late Late Show* and on *Comedy Central*. Colm also set up and runs the @irishmammies Twitter account which is where this whole thing started. It's followed by over 100,000 people and still going strong.

This is his second book. The first - *Isn't It Well For Ye?* - has been on the bestseller lists in Ireland since its publication and was shortlisted for an Irish Book Award.

From Dripsey in County Cork, Colm now lives in Dublin (but gets home when he can, especially as there's a grand road there now).

Also by Colm O'Regan

Isn't It Well For Ye?

The Book of Irish Mammies

Explore the phenomenon of the Irish Mammy and what she might say about everything from the 'new mass' to the cardinal sin of not owning a cough bottle and the importance of airing clothes properly.

So if you're an Irish Mammy, have one, know one or suspect you might be turning into one, this book will act as your guide.

Shortlisted for Best Irish Published Book of the Year at the Irish Book Awards

"A hilarious analysis of the woman in all our lives … It deserves an award just for the title"

Irish Independent

"Isn't he very smart now?
If he was half as smart at his exams …"

Irish Mammy Magazine